A Primer
Guide to
Total
Quality
Management

Larry A. McCloskey &
Dennis N. Collett

Published by GOAL/QPC
13 Branch Street
Methuen, MA 01844-1953
508•685-3900
Fax: 508•685-6151

ISBN 1-879364-35-2

First Edition
10 9 8 7 6 5 4 3 2 1

CONTENTS

ACKNOWLEDGMENTS

This book would not have been possible without the assistance and support of numerous individuals. While the authors could not hope to ever name everyone who provided assistance, we give special thanks to:

Our loving and supportive wives and children, for their patience.

Michael Brassard, for technical assistance and editing.

GOAL/QPC staff, for their review comments.

Bob King, for his willingness to support our vision.

The many business professionals who provided constructive criticism where needed.

The Paperworks (Corvallis, Oregon) for first rate word processing and graphics production.

In the spirit of continuous improvement, we thank in advance all those who will provide recommendations for updates and improvements for the next edition of **TQM, A BASIC TEXT**.

INTRODUCTION

Two years before the first printing the this text, the authors began an intense study of Total Quality Management (TQM), and its pseudonyms and components (Quality Improvement, Statistical Process Control, Quality Circles, etc.). One glaring omission was noticed in the available printed materials—a common language, non-technical overview of TQM. One that described the various "tools" simply and clearly. The kind of text that a fiscally restricted, very small business could study and **APPLY**, without accruing the significant overhead associated with traveling to conferences, or hosting management consultants.

Since both authors are small business owners, the value of such a text was clear. Finding someone sufficiently forward-thinking to support the production and printing, however, appeared to be a major issue. Until that is, GOAL/QPC Executive Director, Bob King agreed to accept that responsibility. With the assurance of publication, dependent only on a quality manuscript, the mission of the text was developed:

THE MISSION OF *TQM, A BASIC TEXT* IS TO PROVIDE A SINGLE VOLUME, COMPREHENSIVE, PLAIN LANGUAGE TEXT DESCRIBING THE ELEMENTS AND TOOLS OF TOTAL QUALITY MANAGEMENT.

We believe that mission has been realized. The information contained in this text will furnish you and/or your organization with an overview of TQM. It describes the data tools of statistical process control, using common business scenarios as illustrations. Examples of the application of the Seven Management and Planning Tools are also provided, each in a simple-language business setting. This is a text that will allow you to understand TQM, and even begin to apply some of the skills which lead to continuous improvement.

Our experience indicates that our readers will see issues addressed, in the book's scenarios, which somewhat parallel existing issues in their own organizations. A possible reaction might be to initiate a process change after reading only one section of the text. We strongly recommend that you read this text completely **BEFORE** modifying any of your existing processes. Supplement your initial knowledge with continued study in the field of continuous-improvement. Effective process modifications are rarely as simplistic as they initially appear. Study completely, **THEN** begin your process improvement plan. Eventually the appropriate action will present itself.

Studying TQM is a massive undertaking. There are a number of consulting organizations in the world that promote Total Quality Management. No two offer exactly the same materials, courses, or consulting formats. Which one is right? The answer is, of course, "all of them." There is no single source of the "right" way to create customer-oriented, continuous improvement in your organization. There is only one source of the "right" information about your organization—that source is you and your organization. No book, no consultant, no guru can give you the solution to your problems.

The solution to your problems is held in the collective minds of your organization. The trick is to find a way to get it out and to use it. A careful study of TQM will reveal that it is an attitude as much as a framework. The biggest obstacle to organizational success is the inability of management to successfully capture the combined wisdom of the organization, and put that wisdom to work. TQM promotes the aggressive solicitation of that wisdom, it provides tools with which the organization can document data, quantify intuition, and create unfailingly appropriate, mission-consistent plans. But, like even the best computer program, it can't create the data, it only helps you process it.

Small and very small businesses, primarily due to fiscal limits, have been unable to afford traditional TQM consulting and training. It is a goal of the authors to create a resource that will allow these entrepreneurs an affordable admission into the world of total quality. This text, and subsequent resources as identified by our customers (you!), are intended to expedite and simplify the move toward quality processes.

Even before the final draft was completed, we began receiving inquiries from college and university business schools, interested in adding **TQM, A BASIC TEXT** to their business libraries, and even using it as a classroom text. To those of you who are formal students of business, we offer this text as an overview of TQM in its current form. No matter what your business-related goals are, an understanding of total quality will be invaluable.

Most modern businesses include in their list of primary criteria for hiring:

- The ability to make good decisions,
- Team-work skills,
- And critical thinking/problem solving skills.

Given those criteria, you may never find a more valuable professional development text than this one. Study the scenarios herein for their **MEANING**. Seek the basic, common thread among each of the sections. Internalize the concepts of quality group interaction, statistically valid data decisions, and strategic planning. Make yourself a valuable commodity to your prospective employer (especially if that's **YOU**).

Teachers—remember, "He who dares to teach must never cease to learn." Education is one of the few common experiences we all share. Help develop students who "meet or exceed" the needs of an ever-changing world; students who can reason critically, think analytically, and care about their brothers and sisters on this planet.

If this text is presented to you by your supervisor or employer; Rejoice! Assuming (s)he has read this text too, you are working for someone who is apparently ready to **TRULY** value you as an important resource for the organization. Your employer has implied your right to be heard in relation to the processes about which you have knowledge, to be a part of the solution to problems that make your work less rewarding, and to learn how to become "all you can be."

You must also accept responsibilities. You have the obligation to do honest, conscientious work, to initiate the investigation of processes you recognize as inefficient or ineffective, and to be a problem-solver rather than a problem-promoter.

The benefits outweigh the difficulties by astronomical proportions.

To those of you who don't fit into any of the mentioned categories, let this text teach you as it has taught the authors. Read, learn, and enjoy a continuously improving life!

TOTAL QUALITY MANAGEMENT
AN OVERVIEW

The American Heritage Dictionary defines **QUALITY** as "excellence, superiority." In America, "quality" has become, too often, an advertising buzz word rather than a sincerely sought after attribute. While many major U.S. manufacturers have begun to swing their ponderous forms toward the quality horizon, there is a long way to go.

TOTAL QUALITY MANAGEMENT (TQM) is, in simplest terms, an enterprise life-style that stresses one single issue: customer satisfaction. TQM is manifested as superior products, excellent service, and rapid adjustment to address ever-changing customer needs.

There is no aspect of customer satisfaction that isn't part of TQM. Virtually any business improvement program is nothing more than some aspect of Total Quality Management.

• TQM is business character. It is not a "flavor of the month" management experiment. A TQM business is TQM from top to bottom, from skin to heart, and from brain to muscle. There is no aspect of a TQM unit that can't be tied to a single vision and mission for that unit.

•A TQM business recognizes that the customer's wants and needs *are* the market, and therefore the only trophy worth seeking. A business' customers include its employees, suppliers, retail purchasers, and the community in which it operates. The decision to become a TQM enterprise should be based on a sincere willingness to create a business with a new "bottom line." The new bottom line is **QUALITY**. The phrases "customer wants" and "customer needs" are equated with quality because quality is what all customers want in every product and service they buy. You can produce a product which is indestructible and inexpensive, but if it isn't something that the customer wants, it won't produce profit. Profit, fortunately, is a natural by-product of true quality, and any business which truly fulfills a customer need/want will achieve financial success. That success, however, is not always immediate. TQM is more like a progressive series of swimming lessons than like a ship's life preserver. The TQM decision should be a refocusing; instead of the traditional, myopic concern of "maximum profits" today, the distant vision of what your business can become tomorrow.

GOAL/QPC has identified a ten element model of **TOTAL QUALITY MANAGEMENT**. The ten elements may also be used as a general guide for implementing TQM in an organization. These 10 elements are summarized in this section as follows.

ELEMENT I
THE TQM DECISION

As discussed above, the decision to implement TQM as a management format in your business should be made after careful study and preparation. It's difficult to maintain a dedication to TQM in an organization if a quick, emotional decision to implement is followed by an equally rapid decline in management enthusiasm about keeping it going. Many TQM texts unequivocally propose that the top level management **MUST** be 100% committed to TQM implementation for the transformation to be successful. While there have been some very successful sub-unit implementations of TQM practices within larger non-TQM organizations, most successful programs do, in fact, begin at the top. A manager's TQM decision should be informed and oriented toward customers and quality. Whether your business is a sole proprietorship or a massive corporate entity, TQM—or any management format—must be an honest commitment.

If your organization is currently enjoying fiscal health, you are in the perfect position to implement TQM. It will allow you to identify where, how, and why you are successful. TQM will empower you to identify future market trends, strengths, and weaknesses in your ability to address future markets; and build-in the capacity to adapt your equipment and personnel to effectively maintain your market position. You may already know from experience that many major U.S. corporations employ TQM practices and require all of their suppliers to exercise quality management as well. This is the natural result of those corporations' recognition of the improved product and service quality that TQM produces. While many new TQM organizations begin to realize measurable improvement within days of initial start-up, full implementation can take as long as five or more years. It's wise to view TQM as an investment and not a quick-fix grant.

A business in financial trouble can also benefit by adopting a Total Quality Management format, though many managers choose to cut funds for training in the first, frantic attempts to control red ink. Training is an integral aspect of TQM implementation. The decision to initiate TQM, for a business in financial trouble, is like the dilemma faced by a group of parched desert travellers upon reaching a hand pump water well. Should you divvy the small amount of water in the primer can, or pour it down the pump shaft in hopes that it will prime the pump and produce all the water you really want? It's a difficult decision to make when no one can produce a guarantee of success for the investment. A careful perusal of this text, however, may produce the level of confidence you need to invest your waning resources to prime the deep spring of your future.

ELEMENT II
CUSTOMER FOCUS

For too many years, some of us have considered our customers as simply the original source of our profit. If we could get them to let go of some of the contents of their wallets, we have been successful. Fortunately, that shortsighted philosophy is dying. An increasing awareness of the need to truly *serve* our customers is becoming an American tradition.

TQM training promotes, throughout an organization, the reality of producing customer satisfaction. From research and development through sales and service, every employee orients her/his efforts toward pleasing the customer. Customer input is sought at every level. No change is made unless it can be illustrated as a move toward increased customer satisfaction. A clear documentation of customer dissatisfaction results in a careful evaluation of business processes, followed by a decisive and deliberate modification of those processes to better meet, and then exceed the customer's quality requirements. While some organizations seek to fulfill the basic level of quality—what the customer *must* have or expects—TQM businesses seek the highest level of quality by setting new and exciting standards in their field of endeavor.

TQM education includes instruction in the use of various tools which can be applied to turn customer demands into daily work assignments from the executive offices to the factory floor. The two tools' sections in this text, Quality Control (QC) Tools and Management and Planning (MP) Tools, will define the tools, as well as a variety of sample applications for each. The tool sets are as potentially valuable to very small businesses as they have proven to be for industrial giants around the globe. With an awareness of the mandate of pleasing one's customers and means of initiating the changes needed to accomplish that mandate, a TQM organization is well prepared for the future.

ELEMENT III
CRITICAL PROCESSES (CP'S)

The term "Critical Processes" is self-explanatory. They are the general tasks or procedures that you *must* accomplish to achieve success in your endeavors. They can be distilled to 5 or 10 concise statements which account for nearly all of the factors of success for your specific position. Every position in your organization has critical processes. The executive officer's CP's may sound quite general compared to those of a factory worker, but each must accomplish his/her CP's in order to be successful at that particular position. The total combination of line workers' CP's, once accomplished, should constitute a significant portion of the CP's of their supervisor. If all the line supervisors complete their critical processes, the next level of managers' CP's should therefore be favorably impacted, and so on to the top executive. The executive officer's CP's, once accomplished, assure success of the entire organization.

There are specific MP tools which can be applied to identify the critical processes of every member in your organization. Not surprisingly, the starting point in the development of CP's is "identifying your customers." Internal customers (employees, other divisions, etc.), as well as the traditional external customers are considered in the development of an organization's critical processes. Once all customers are documented, their needs are identified and grouped by more general patterns or themes. These general themes are evaluated to determine which tasks each level must accomplish in order to fulfill those customer needs. A more detailed procedure for identifying your own critical processes is found on pages 68-71 of this text.

Anyone can benefit from the identification of critical processes, whether they relate to personal or professional activities. Whether an organization decides to incorporate a formal TQM format or not, the identification of critical processes can illuminate the sometimes surprising discrepancy between what one does and what one should be doing to accomplish goals.

ELEMENT IV
INITIAL TEAMS

If your business involves more than one person, you will benefit from the productivity of team processes. In a large organization, the CEO may identify senior-level managers from various divisions as members of an Executive Steering Committee (ESC). The ESC will identify areas of critical importance, including an implementation strategy, and problems that need immediate resolution. In a smaller business, your ESC may be made-up of all your supervisors, or even all your employees.

The initial projects that your ESC identifies should be those with the highest potential for organizational benefit, that have a good chance of success, and that will be highly visible. Each of these project characteristics will increase the opportunity to build momentum into a TQM implementation.

Once the ESC has identified the general project issues that will be addressed, down-line teams are formed to further plan and subsequently carry out the specifics of the projects. There are two primary types of project teams.

1. Functional teams: A functional team is composed of members who perform a similar function in an organization. In a small business it may not be possible to form functional teams, due to the fact that each function in the business is carried out by only one person. In larger organizations, functional teams are used to evaluate and deal with issues that are specific to that group. While both types of teams, as a result of the members' TQM training, are constantly aware of the impact of their deci-

sions on other divisions, the functional team members tend to initiate changes within their own operating area. A functional team is usually an ongoing, permanent group and will constantly study issues affecting their processes.

2. Cross-functional teams: As you might have guessed, a cross-functional team is composed of members who represent a variety of functions or divisions. For example, a cross-functional team might include one member from research and development, one from design, a manufacturing representative, and a sales person. Even though your organization may employ only four or five people, you can effectively utilize this team format. Unlike the functional team, the cross-functional team is usually ad hoc, or brought together to deal with a specific issue. The ESC, if performing effectively, should serve the function of an ongoing cross-functional team, and should be able to effectively determine the composition needed for situational cross-functional teams.

For a team to function effectively, all members should be educated in the use of the two sets of tools described in this text. By educating all members of your organization in the use of the tools, you are preparing each and every member of your organization to be an effective team member. The most successful organizations in the world are those that have recognized the value of each employee's ideas. Every person in your organization has a unique and valuable perspective, one which might create a whole new future for your organization. Training and supporting your employees, as well as creating a fear-free organizational structure increases the probability that each employee will have the opportunity and motivation to drive your organization to success.

ELEMENT V
THE FIVE-YEAR PLAN

Your organization may choose a three, four, or five year, long-range planning format. Regardless of the period you select, the concept of long range planning is an integral part of the TQM concept. The five-year plan may address specific information relating to your company's future market share, introduction of new products, cost efficiency, and improved mechanization and processes.

While conventional methods of planning often involve planning one year at a time, beginning with this year and progressing forward, based on what might be accomplished in the next 12 months, TQM planning looks far into the future and identifies what you can become; then provides a framework in which you systematically identify each step you'll need to take to get there. It's very difficult, after all, to get to your destination if you don't first identify it!

Every organization should have a clear, printed statement of **WHAT** it looks like when it is performing at the level of **PERFECTION**. That statement is known as an organizational **VISION**. Your vision statement should be written in present tense, " We are..." as opposed to "We will be..." The vision statement is an opportunity to see your organization as everything it can be. Every aspect of every plan and every process should be supportable as a step toward the realization of the organization's vision. If any action you or your business takes cannot be supported as a move toward your vision, it's counter-productive. If your business doesn't already have a formal vision, several of the management and planning tools will be helpful in preparing one.

Another basic element of a TQM organization's format is the organizational **MISSION** statement. The mission of an organization is more detailed than its vision, and addresses the customers you serve, which of their need(s) you will meet/exceed, and generally how that will be accomplished. It is, in essence, **A STATEMENT OF THE ORGANIZATION'S PURPOSE FOR EXISTING**. One of the most beneficial aspects of a clear mission statement is the way it allows an organization to focus its energy. By identifying what you do, its much less likely that you'll get bogged down in a project which moves you away from your vision. Too many organizations waste time trying to be everything to everyone. No business has ever, or likely will ever, accomplish that. You are far better off doing what you do best, and concentrating your efforts on that. The term "cutting edge" is frequently used to describe organizations that are consistently the first in their field to develop new ideas or products. As the term implies, those organizations are finely sharpened to apply the greatest energy to the smallest point of resistance.

The five-year plan includes a small number of intermediate goals. A one-year plan is prepared at the same time as the five-year plan. It identifies more immediate goals which must be accomplished to move your business toward its five-year goals. The one-year goals should be the most immediately needed and most critical issues facing your organization. As you would expect, these goals are analyzed to identify exactly what every member of your organization must accomplish to attain them. The specific tasks that **MUST** be accomplished for each level, in TQM jargon, are known as the target actions (better known as **HOSHIN** items in many TQM texts) for that level. Identifying these critical break-through items can also be accomplished through appropriate application of the Management and Planning Tools. You'll learn more about this process in a later section of this text. Element VII in this TQM overview also deals with Hoshin planning.

ELEMENT VI
MANAGING TQM MOMENTUM

Unlike the preceding five elements, this and the next four elements are ongoing activities in a mature TQM environment. They can begin at the very initiation of the TQM implementation, and should continue forever as elements of an effective organization.

The primary obligation for managing the momentum of a growing TQM culture belongs to the chief executive, whether that person is a corporate CEO or a local shoe store owner. If the organization is large enough to accommodate an ESC, the chief executive will delegate a major part of the obligation to that group. Regardless of who is in charge, the management role involves the evaluation of team efficiency and the effectiveness of the organization's activities. Coordination of team activities, fostering an open environment which empowers employees, and providing appropriate recognition and reward for success are all important aspects of continued management of TQM.

Momentum should involve an aggressive program to provide training for all personnel in the use of the tools, as well as effective communication skills. Every member of the organization should be regularly updated about organizational successes, revisions in plans, and the activities of groups and teams. One of the basic tenets of a TQM business is the recognition of the value of the individual employee. It is the employees who will make an organization successful, and it is the employees who should be applauded and rewarded when those successes occur. Managing a successful TQM business means making sure the employees have everything they need to help the business succeed.

ELEMENT VII
BREAKTHROUGH PLANNING (HOSHIN)

In a preceding part of this overview (Element V), the term Hoshin was introduced. A rough translation of this Japanese term is **TARGET**. An organization's Hoshin flows from the five-year plan, and is an issue that is most urgent and critical. A Hoshin item is an issue or problem which has a relatively short projected time frame for resolution, as a general rule one year or less, and has a high potential impact on the organization. By applying various tools and effective analysis procedures, the organization's progress toward the Hoshin is evaluated at least quarterly. Division and individual processes can be appropriately modified to guarantee that the organization is continuing to move directly toward the accomplishment of the Hoshin.

The concept of review is a basic step in the continuous improvement TQM "walk." All processes are reviewed on a regular basis, utilizing the **PLAN-DO-CHECK-ACT** or **PDCA** format. All managers, or even all employees in a small organization, utilize this PDCA process throughout the Hoshin development and activity. Traditional TQM material depicts the PDCA as a circle (Figure 1).

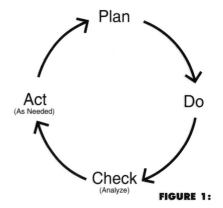

FIGURE 1:

The PDCA circle illustrates the constant improvement nature of TQM. All processes are under constant evaluation, and therefore constant improvement. When a significant improvement in a process is identified, the PDCA circle is modified to standardize the improvement. Standardizing allows an organization an opportunity to incorporate an improvement from one area into the process of all similar areas. Improved quality processes are too valuable to use on a limited basis. A more detailed description of the PDCA circle is in Appendix C.

The Hoshin aspect of the TQM implementation process is a "from the top, down" process. It is the boss' obligation, whether through an ESC or personally, to identify her/his breakthrough issues for the organization. The next level of managers or employees cannot identify their own Hoshins until they are fully informed of the chief executive's. These second level managers' Hoshins are the most important tasks that they must complete to allow the chief executive the support (s)he needs to complete his/hers.

The process of identifying the organization's Hoshins, and subsequently other downline personnel's Hoshins requires conscientious communication on both planes, horizontal (people or divisions involved in similar functions) as well as vertical (those divisions of people involved in processes that precede or follow your own). Functional and cross-functional teams, obviously, play an important role in this process. By the end of a thorough Hoshin planning process, every employee should be able to identify the organization's Hoshin, and the tasks that (s)he must accomplish to allow the Hoshin to be achieved. The Hoshin planning process itself is an exercise which fosters a positive, creative, focusing work environment.

ELEMENT VIII
DAILY MANAGEMENT

As the term implies, daily management is the process of turning the generalities of the CEO's Hoshins and five-year objectives into the specifics of what should employee "A" do right now!

Daily management allows all employees to function at their highest level of efficiency by maximizing the accuracy of their perception of the tasks they must perform. A moving company employee, for example, is less likely to break clients' dishes if he is given specific directions about how to pack the dishes, and more likely to break the dishes if he is simple told, "Don't break any dishes!" Only by carefully managing activities on a daily basis can an organization effectively evolve at the pace necessary to survive in today's rapidly changing world market.

As in preceding steps, daily management involves constant **PLAN-DO-CHECK-ACT** and **STANDARDIZATION** of improved processes. All members of the organization regularly utilize the tools to provide clear and useful data about the operation of their division or job.

All changes developed through the PDCA process are carefully tied to the satisfaction of the customer. In the case of a large or multi-level organization, other divisions and employees are also "customers" who deserve consideration when changes are being considered which might affect their endeavors. Cross-functional teams are employed to assure that this "impact forecasting" takes place adequately.

Daily management is the individual fiber from which the organizational Hoshin and long-range objectives are woven. Carefully planned and conscientiously carried out daily tasks assure the satisfaction of the customers, which include every member of the organization. (See also Daily Management, page 125.)

ELEMENT IX
NEW TEAMS

As a TQM organization matures, it naturally begins to involve as many employees as possible in teams. The perfect organization would provide regular forums for every employee so that her/his perspectives and recommendations about issues that affect them are heard. If, as an executive or manager, you understand that every individual employee has value far beyond the performance of the assigned job tasks, you realize the investment that teams constitute in the organization. Even if you have only one employee, you should recognize the potential gold mine that exists between the ears of that individual.

The application of functional teams within a division, and cross-functional teams across divisions are the trademark of an organization which appropriately prizes the minds of its workers. It also improves employee "buy in" to new processes and methods because they, themselves, had a voice in the decision.

Some managers complain that a team of five employees "costs" as much as $100 to $200 per hour (depending on salary) while meeting.

The improved morale and increased sense of empowerment for the employees should be worth that much to a forward thinking manager; not to mention the fact that one large-scale process improvement could save the manager many times that sum. By the time an organization matures through the initiation of a TQM format of business, the value of teams should be beyond question.

ELEMENT X
EVALUATE PROCESSES

Functioning TQM is a constant process of evaluation. All processes are under regular observation with the Quality Control Tools. The Management and Planning Tools provide for the translation of ideas into usable data. The TQM process utilizes both tool products to improve processes as needed. The concept of evaluation is an integral aspect of daily management for every member of the organization.

There are also more formalized evaluations taking place at regular intervals. All managers' Hoshin reports are reviewed by the ESC on a quarterly basis. At the end of the year, the final Hoshin evaluation is completed and the next year's Hoshin is identified.

The Hoshin, you recall, is the most imperative objective of the five year, long-range plan. The completion of the first year automatically requires the development of a new fifth year for the long-range plan.

The annual review provides the CEO with feedback relating to employee training needs and, possibly, motivation for employees relating to their involvement in the organization's management operations. It is the top level mandate to promote a forward looking, constant improvement atmosphere that motivates and enables all members of the organization to be involved, productive partners.

TOOL BAG #1 - THE QUALITY CONTROL TOOLS

The tools described in this section are generally referred to as the Quality Control or QC Tools. As described in the TQM overview, all processes are in a constant state of fluctuation or change. Managing your business as a constantly improving, quality oriented entity requires that you be able to quickly and efficiently utilize all available data. The data must be carefully captured, analyzed, and clearly displayed to be of greatest utility. This section describes eight statistical tools:

1. The Check Sheet
2. The Flow Chart
3. The Descending Bar Chart (Pareto Chart)
4. The Fishbone Chart (The Cause and Effect Chart)
5. The Run Chart
6. The Barbell Chart (Histogram)
7. The Scatter Diagram
8. The Control Chart

    Each of these eight tools can be used to illustrate data created by virtually any size or type of process. Whether you operate a sole proprietor business in your home, or manage a Fortune 500 corporation, these tools should be in regular use in your organization. The QC Tools are easy to understand, simple to use, and time-tested in a wide variety of applications. Once you're familiar with the QC Tools you'll find them indispensable, whether for monitoring a process to identify problems, or for resolving problems once they have been identified. You may be surprised at the simplicity of some of the tools. You very likely already employ some of the QC Tools, though most non-TQM organizations don't employ them to as great a benefit as they could. Use of these tools alone, however, doesn't constitute a Total Quality Management organizational style. They are, however, the foundation of the statistical control every organization needs to foster an environmental culture in which quality can grow.

THE CHECK SHEET

I f you have ever kept informal score at a basketball game or documented the number of times a speaker says "Uh," you probably used a tally sheet or check sheet. The quality control check sheet is very similar to that informal game tally, except that it is rarely constructed on an empty popcorn bag.

A check sheet is a simple means of documenting information about samples from a process. This tool is one that is useful as part of an ongoing monitoring mechanism, as well as a starting point in the investigation of suspected process problems.

As an ongoing monitoring tool, the check sheet is frequently used to chart characteristics of samples taken from a production line. When applied as a starting point in a system investigation, the check sheet is used to determine if identifiable patterns exist which might indicate a process deficiency. Both applications produce the same basic kind of data: what variations does the process create and how often does each variation occur?

A micro brewer needs to evaluate the consistency of its beer flavor from batch to batch The brew master samples every batch and evaluates it relating to flavor characteristics. He might apply a check sheet which looks like this:

THE BREWMASTER'S CHECK SHEET

FLAVOR DEFECT	JANUARY			
	WEEK 1	WEEK 2	WEEK 3	TOTAL
TOO FLAT	I	II	I	**4**
TOO BITTER	THL I	IIII	THL	15
TOO HAZY	II	III	I	6
TOO MUCH CARBONATION		II		2
TOO WATERY	I	III	III	7

FIGURE 2:

The brewmaster's check sheet displays the traditional elements of a complete check sheet.

- Clear indication of the time frame involved (the month of January)

- The specific indicators of deficiency are stated (too bitter, too hazy, etc.)

- The check sheet is clearly labeled and has enough room to accommodate the number of tallies necessary.

- There is a consistent method for securing the samples.

The brewmaster tastes the brew at the top of each keg, tastes all samples at the same temperature, and clears his palate with the same food. Since the brewery is very small, and produces brews from only one production line, one check sheet is all he needs. If the brewmaster worked in a larger brewery, he would have to apply a different check sheet for each production line. That would guarantee that he could identify specific characteristics of each line and not change the processes of all the lines in an attempt to remedy a problem in a single line of production.

With the information on the brewmaster's check sheet, he is able to clearly observe a frequent taste deficiency relating to bitterness. He will research his brew notes and determine what variations there might be in the hops used in each of the brew batches. A carefully studied analysis should allow him to make calculated changes in his hop use. In so doing, he's saved the brewery a time consuming and expensive trial and error resolution of the problem.

In a larger scale production business, sampling may involve the inspection of one unit for every thousand units produced. In this application there are additional factors to consider in the sampling procedure.

- The method of securing samples should be as **simple** and **streamlined** as possible. This increases the probability that the samples are not from an abnormal process, and also improves the overall effectiveness of the use of personnel time.

- All sample evaluators must have a **consistent perception of what is being measured**, and how it is being measured.

- Be sure to make the **samples as typical** of the process as possible.

     The check sheet is often the initial step in securing data which will be better illustrated with other tools; The descending bar chart, and the barbell chart for example. Each of these tools is described later in this section. While other tools are more effective visual representations of sample data, the modest check sheet is frequently the tool of choice to initially investigate a process and document the sample variations.

THE FLOW CHART

■ ■ ■ ■ ■ ■

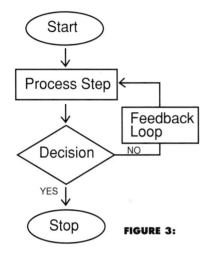

FIGURE 3:

Considered one of the simplest tools, the flow chart can be as basic or technically intricate as the process it's used to illustrate. The flow chart is used to provide a visual representation of any progressive process. Each type of process step is traditionally identified on the chart by a standarized geometric shape (see Figure 3).

A flow chart illustrates a process from start to finish, and should include every step in between. A process which includes alternative routes of reaction to a particular action will be flow charted to portray each alternative. Since most processes are not as simple and linear as the basic illustration seen in Figure 3, the average flow chart will appear more complex than this sample. For example, even a process as rudimentary as getting dressed in the morning may become complicated by variables.

A WARDROBE SELECTION

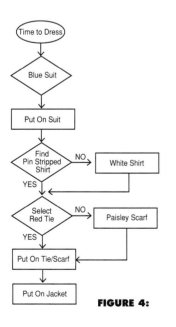

FIGURE 4:

Rebecca selected a navy blue suit for work attire. She selected her plain red tie and began pushing aside hanger after hanger, looking for her pin-striped shirt. Unable to find it, she opted for a white blouse. Since she was to wear an unpatterned blouse, she chose a yellow paisley scarf in place of the solid red tie. A flow chart of this clothes selection process looks like Figure 4.

Every process has a "perfect" path. Unfortunately, not everything in life proceeds as planned. While it's usually easy to tell that something has gone wrong in a process, it's not always so easy to determine what went wrong, and at what point. One of the most common uses of the flow chart is the analysis of a process for weaknesses or stumbling points.

By taking the time to assemble people directly involved in each step of a process, a manager can facilitate the construction of a flow chart for that process. With people present who are intimately involved in each step, a process can be effectively critiqued utilizing a set of flow charts. The first chart the group may choose to construct is a "perfect" process flow chart. The manager may be surprised to find that the perfect process, from the perspective of the production people, is different from the process the manager has been trying to put in place. Once a realistic, perfect flow chart is constructed, the same people should construct a flow chart of the process as it actually takes place. A careful comparison of the two should illuminate existing strengths and weaknesses in the current process, as well as changes that can be made to remedy those weaknesses. A basic difficulty in preparing a "perfect" flow chart is our tendency to think in terms of our experience. We sometimes tend to think of every alternative as some variation of the process we've used before. During the production of the "perfect" flow chart, allow some latitude for original, non-traditional possibilities. Allow logic and creativity to balance equally.

Virtually any process can be charted in this fashion. The steps involved in the manufacturing of a hammer, the path of a purchase order, the creation of a bronze sculpture can all be flow charted.

Frequently, a larger process will involve parallel, smaller processes. The initial sub-processes in the overall task of making a loaf of bread, for example, include scalding the milk and dissolving the yeast in warm water. In real life we don't usually complete one such task before beginning another, so a flow chart of such a process should reflect that real-life overlapping of steps (Figure 5).

QUICKER BREAD DOUGH

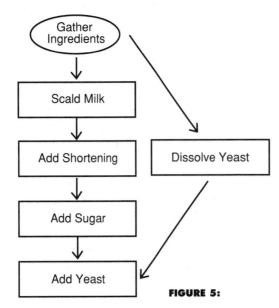

FIGURE 5:

A flow chart is also an excellent tool to assist in making decisions about alternatives to a current process. A financial institution, for example, may be interested in reviewing its method of processing loan applications, due to customer complaints about having to make several calls or trips to the institution to sign forms, provide additional information, etc. A flow chart of the current loan application process could be constructed, allowing the loan officials to identify potential areas for improvement in the process steps. Such a flow chart might look like Figure 6.

LOAN PROCESS OPTIONS

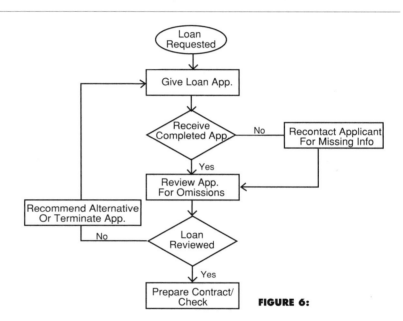

FIGURE 6:

The loan department employees identified as a common task the issue of soliciting additional information from the loan applicant. That consideration is added onto the flow chart as a "feedback loop." Their "perfect" process chart did not include this step. In addition, they determine that deleting that step would put the institution closer to addressing the primary loan applicant complaint: having to recontact the institution after submitting the initial application. The loan department personnel determined they could resolve most of these delays by asking the applicant to stay at the loan department while someone conducted a cursory review of the application. Most post-application recontacts, the loan officers advised, involved the resolution of simple issues such as a missing signature, an incomplete address, etc., most of which could be solicited from the applicant before (s)he left.

The flow chart is a simple and very flexible tool. There are few absolute rules regarding it's application, but here are a few recommendations:

- While you may choose to employ different geometric symbols for your own flow charts from the ones displayed in this section, be sure to consistently use the same symbols for the same process steps. If your chart displays more than one arrow *out* of a process step box, you may need a decision diamond at that location. This helps to identify the preferred of two or more alternatives, rather than implying that all are worth equal consideration. Be certain to clearly identify the process under consideration, including clear start and stop points.

- Seek input from each unit involved in a particular process. A manager's perception of how things get done down-line may not be consistent with that unit's actual process.

- Make your feedback loops a realistic representation of your process. Don't indicate that defective parts are sent to the laboratory for analysis if they are, in fact, usually discarded.

DESCENDING BAR CHART (PARETO CHART)

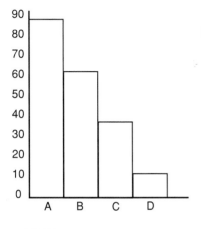

FIGURE 7:

The Descending Bar Chart (DBC). This tool is a simple, easy to understand method of illustrating the relative importance or frequency of different factors. It is simple to construct, easy to understand, and very effective in helping you decide what aspects of a process may be causing the biggest problems. The Descending Bar Chart is also known as the Pareto (Pä-rá-to) Chart among TQM aficionados. The only difference between a DBC and the bar graphs you used to construct in school is the order in which you place the bars. The tallest bar (most frequently occurring factor) is placed at the far left, at the junction of the horizontal and vertical graph axes. The next tallest bar is on the immediate right of the tallest one, and so on down the line. When you're done placing your data on a DBC, you'll have a set of stair steps with the top of the stairs on the left, and the bottom on the right (Figure 7).

There is one data bar which should be placed at the far right side of the stairs, regardless of its height. That's the "other" or "miscellaneous" category, a combination of unknown or statistically insignificant data that are displayed to illustrate the comparative relationship of the other data bars to all, similarly known

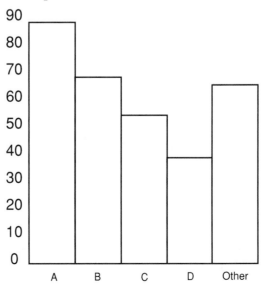

FIGURE 8:

data. As a general rule, that category will be relatively small; and in virtually every case it will be insufficiently defined to allow you to control it (until you can later identify its components). To keep it from interfering with the ranking of factors that you can identify, place it as the last bar, at the far right of the chart (Figures 8 and 9).

While the DBC may initially seem like a tool that's too basic to be of real value, the appropriate application of a series of DBC's to a single problem may help to identify factors in a manner which you hadn't previously considered.

Perhaps the most obvious application of DBC's is in the manufacturing arena. Illustrating the frequency of various types of defects which results in the rejection of products, determining which shift produces the most defective parts, and similar production control applications account for some of the most common uses of this tool (Figures 9 and 10).

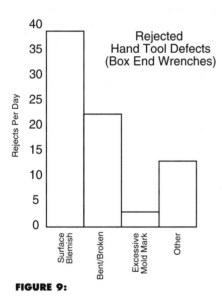

FIGURE 9:

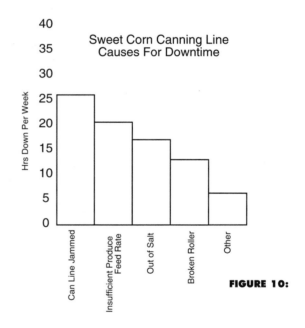

FIGURE 10:

The DBC, however, has applications in virtually every business setting. In the field of law enforcement, for example, the DBC has literally thousands of possible uses.

POLICE SHIFT ASSIGNMENTS

The effective allocation of manpower over three or four shifts requires immense scheduling coordination. The chief or sheriff generally want to have the greatest number of officers on the road during the period when the greatest demands for service are received. The most commonly used method of determining that information is to simply count the total number of calls for service during each shift for a week or a month, and compare the total numbers for each shift. A DBC illustrating that data might look like Figure 11.

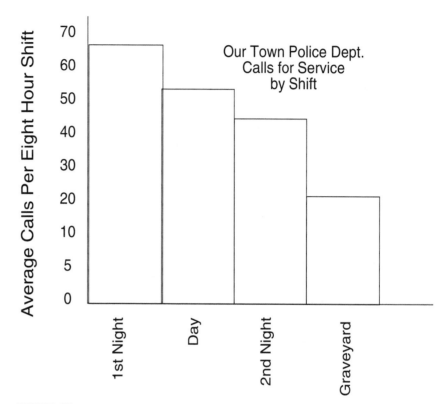

FIGURE 11:

The sheriff or chief might want to analyze the available data further and determine, perhaps, if each shift responds to the same kinds of calls for service. A quick review of most police agency data reports would reveal data that could be used to produce other DBC's which might look like Figures 12 through 15.

Yet another step that the astute administrator might consider is the amount of time an officer generally spends at each kind of call for service. Assembling that data may take some time if the agency hasn't traditionally captured that specific information, but the product could be well worth the effort. The resulting DBC might appear like Figure 16.

In this illustration, the administrator finds that the second night and graveyard shifts are regularly involved with calls that require large amounts of officer time per call. Had the administra-

OUR TOWN POLICE DEPT.
CALLS FOR SERVICE BY TYPE

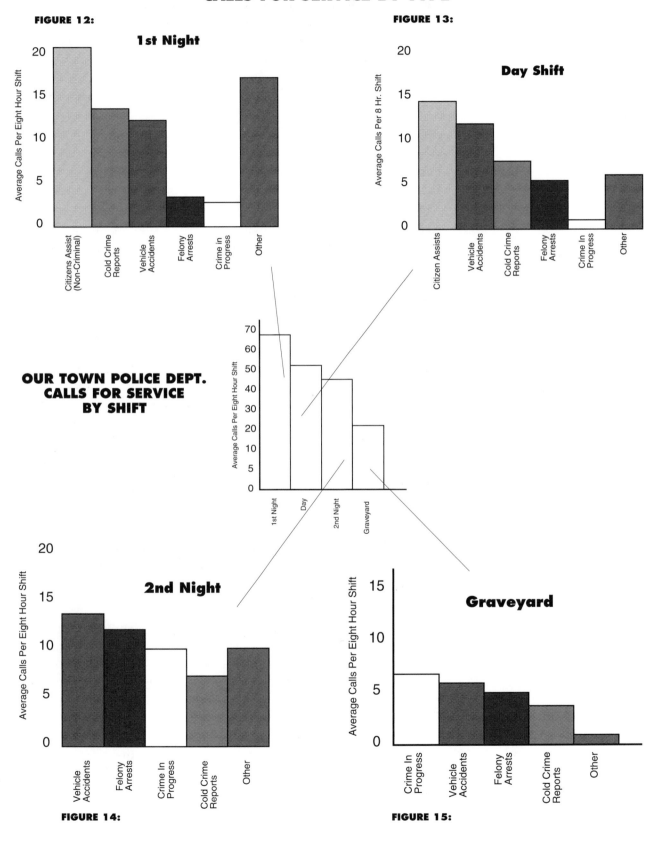

FIGURE 12:

1st Night

Average Calls Per Eight Hour Shift

Citizens Assist (Non-Criminal) · Cold Crime Reports · Vehicle Accidents · Felony Arrests · Crime in Progress · Other

FIGURE 13:

Day Shift

Average Calls Per 8 Hr. Shift

Citizen Assists · Vehicle Accidents · Cold Crime Reports · Felony Arrests · Crime In Progress · Other

OUR TOWN POLICE DEPT.
CALLS FOR SERVICE
BY SHIFT

Average Calls Per Eight Hour Shift

1st Night · Day · 2nd Night · Graveyard

2nd Night

Average Calls Per Eight Hour Shift

Vehicle Accidents · Felony Arrests · Crime In Progress · Cold Crime Reports · Other

FIGURE 14:

Graveyard

Average Calls Per Eight Hour Shift

Crime In Progress · Vehicle Accidents · Felony Arrests · Cold Crime Reports · Other

FIGURE 15:

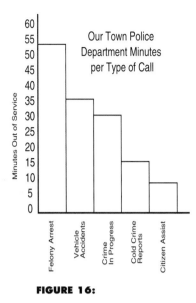

FIGURE 16:

tor made a decision to distribute officers based only on the actual number of calls per shift, second night and graveyard shifts would have been understaffed.

By considering the additional values of call type and duration, the boss is able to come to a completely different conclusion than (s)he would have had (s)he simply relied on the total number of calls as her/his only source of data.

The "Our Town" police department example shows that simple numerical frequency can be misleading. By using tools (in this case the descending bar chart) to investigate and illustrate subsets of the original data, the user may find previously unrecognized patterns. Collecting and analyzing such data will usually require far less time than would be required to "fix" the initial distribution, had it been made using only the basic call frequency data.

TRAINING TO REDUCE SCHOOL LIABILITY

A school district, for example, might identify topics for employee training based on the frequency that the district receives complaints or criticism on various issues. If a superintendent were to request a summary of public complaints by topic, (s)he might receive a DBC that looks something like Figure 17.

Based on the raw frequency data, the superintendent could reasonably conclude that, in order to meet the needs of the district's "customers," the district should provide in-service training with emphasis on the topics of:

- Helping students learn to be accepting of one another
- Developing a desirable teaching style and attitudes
- Developing effective student-progress reports.

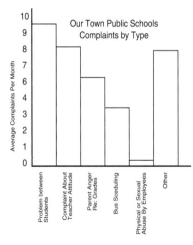

FIGURE 17:

Should the same superintendent choose to quantify each complaint topic in terms of the financial liability potential each problem area creates for the district, the DBC would probably take on a whole new personality (see Figure 18).

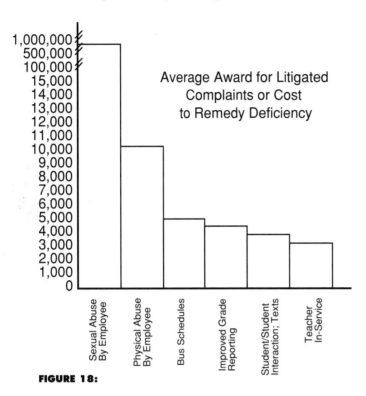

FIGURE 18:

With this data in hand, the administrator might choose to consider training relating to the recognition and reporting of physical and sexual abuse.

Any single issue may lend itself to evaluation from many different perspectives. The simple descending bar chart can initiate a very distinctive and innovative process of problem resolution.

Some things to keep in mind about the DBC:

1. Clearly mark the vertical and horizontal axes of each chart to identify measurement factors and increments.

2. Maintain an open mind. Consider group processes such as brainstorming as a source of chart formats. A member of an assembly group may have a valuable DBC idea that the design department never would have thought of.

3. Consider identifying the percentage that each bar represents of all elements considered. For example, while charting the source of your daily calorie intake of 3000 calories, you might determine that 2100 of those calories were consumed as carbohydrates. On the DBC of your calorie intake by food type, you'd put "70%" (2100 divided by 3000) above the carbohydrate bar (Figure 19).

4. Don't feel as though the DBC tool is going to control your decision-making creativity. It is simply a **TOOL** which you can employ to whatever purpose or end you choose. Your decisions, of course, will be most effective when they are well informed and responsive to known data.

5. When preparing a series of DBC's on chart paper for a group presentation, color each element the same color in every DBC (see Figures 12, 13, 14, 15, on page 26).

6. Be creative with this and all the Quality Control Tools.

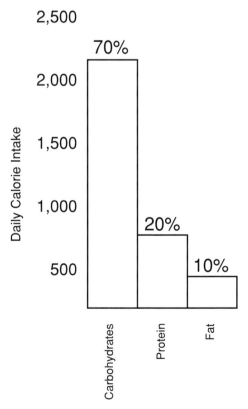

FIGURE 19:

THE FISHBONE DIAGRAM
■ ■ ■ ■ ■ ■

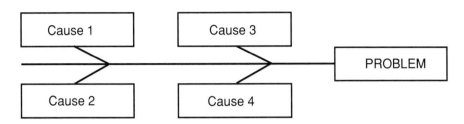

FIGURE 20:

T he fishbone diagram is also known as the cause and effect diagram. It's primarily used to track down the root "cause" of a known problem (effect). It methodically provides the answer to the general question, "What, in all the things we do, could be causing this problem?" Once the general "cause" is identified, begin asking "why?" Why does cause 1 happen; why cause 2? By continuously investigating the "why" for each "cause," the root cause may be more concisely identified.

Applying a fishbone analysis at the point one discovers a problem can save you vast amounts of time in the long run. The true root cause of a problem is not always the obvious option. Should you simply react to symptoms of a problem, you'll need to continually modify your processes in attempts to remedy the unpredictable effects of the unknown. Resolution of the base cause, once identified, could provide a permanent "fix" for a series of annoying problems.

The traditional construction of the fishbone involves identifying the "effect," or symptom, on the right side of the diagram. The primary cause categories are identified through group brainstorming or application of data from a series of check sheets, and placed to the left of the problem (Figure 20).

Commonly used "cause" categories for a manufacturing organization are **METHOD, PEOPLE, MATERIAL**, and **MACHINERY** (3 "M's" and a "P"). These four are traditional cause categories used when searching for root causes of problems

related to the production of material goods. If you are an administrator or manager, you may choose a set of categories which more
appropriately apply to your standard areas of direct control.
Traditional administrative cause categories are **POLICIES,
PROCEDURES, PEOPLE**, and **PLANT** (the 4 P's). Whether you
use one of these traditional sets or develop your own customized
categories, the categories you select should reflect the nature of
your operation, and be sufficiently general to allow you to keep
the number of cause categories to about four. If you find that you
have too many categories, you can probably combine two or more
related categories to reduce the total number.

FAMILY AUTO REPAIR SHOP

For the purpose of illustration, consider an automobile
repair shop with a problem involving frequent customer complaints about the amount of time they have to wait at the front
counter to receive their billing and to get the keys to their cars.
The owner/manager has tried applying the standard fixes to such
problems. He's yelled at the mechanics to get their labor and parts
forms filled out immediately after repairs are completed, he's
cajoled his wife/receptionist to try a "teensy bit" harder to get the
labor and parts forms totaled more rapidly. He even hired his 16
year old daughter, Erin, to work after school, admonishing her to
"help out anywhere you see there's a need." Isn't it amazing that,
as owner of the business, he's asked his daughter to, in essence,
identify and solve his problem?

Fortunately, his daughter is familiar with the fishbone
diagram, having learned about the QC Tools in her economics
class. Erin prepares the following diagram and suggests that mom
and dad sit down with her and apply the tool to the problems at
the shop.

Dad's initial response is to remind Erin that, "We're dealing
with the real world here, Honey, but thanks for your interest."
Erin has also learned something about persuasive argument, and
eventually manages to get both parents to sit down and review
her diagram. Jointly, the family adds the next level of data to
Erin's chart by posing the question, "What are the processes in
each of the major categories that have some effect on the specific
problem (customers have to wait too long when they come to pick
up their cars)?" The resulting additions produce the diagram
below (Figure 21).

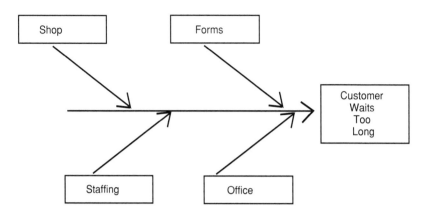

FIGURE 21:

Finally, Erin informs her parents that they need to ask, in relation to each of the previously added issues, "What factors in this process create problems?" The final fishbone diagram looked like Figure 22.

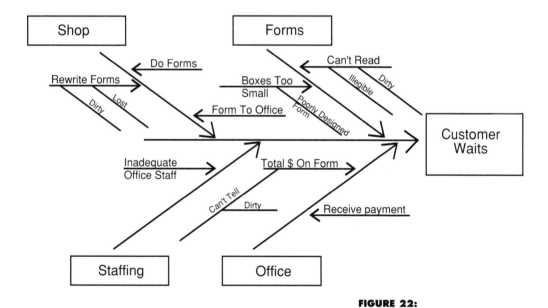

FIGURE 22:

To evaluate the final diagram, look initially for factors that appear in more than one of the four major categories. In this example the problem of soiled or illegible forms appears in three of the four categories. By simply illustrating frequently recurring problems, a fishbone diagram may display recognizable patterns or obviously abnormal combinations of factors, all of which may be used as a starting point for further investigation or action.

Dad's assumption that people weren't completing the forms rapidly enough doesn't seem to be as important a factor as the time that's being lost rewriting and processing the completed forms that are too soiled to read. Several possible remedies to the newly identified base cause will be considered and resolution will be simple and inexpensive.

The process of constructing a fishbone may also, as in this case, raise questions that can identify data that would be helpful in further analyses. How many customer complaints are received from customers who arrive with the "rush" at 5:00 each afternoon? How much time is reasonable for a customer to wait? How long have complaining customers had to wait? Having recognized the importance of these forms of information, all employees will be sensitive to the need to capture and record it in the future. The billing/customer receipt form may even be modified to include a customer response form.

Dad's initial recognition of the problem was via the "gut reaction" technique. Moving from that level of recognition to the final identification and resolution of the root cause is the purpose of the fishbone diagram.

ANALYZING A VALVE LEAK

A valve manufacturer begins to experience an increasing number of returned, defective valves. In order to provide a more consistently acceptable product for his customers, he initiated a more intensive process for testing valves before they were shipped to customers. While this procedure will probably reduce the number of customer complaints, it will do little to solve the real problem—the production of defective valves. The ever increasing size of the pile of discarded, defective valves will serve as a constant reminder of the waste that ineffective processes guarantee.

By applying the traditional 3 M's and a P to a fishbone, his bookkeeper approached the boss with the basic diagram and suggested they work on it together for a while. After a few minutes it became obvious that they needed the input of people from planning and design, as well as production and sales. The bookkeeper suggested they form a team comprised of members of each group and meet again to work on the fishbone.

The team members were identified and assembled. They produced flow charts, check sheets, and descending bar charts at the direction of the bookkeeper. A variety of surprising issues began to surface, but the most immediately valuable information was the identification of a single type of defect that accounted for nearly 60% of all returned, defective valves. Using that specific defect, leakage from around the valve stem, the team constructed the following fishbone (Figure 23).

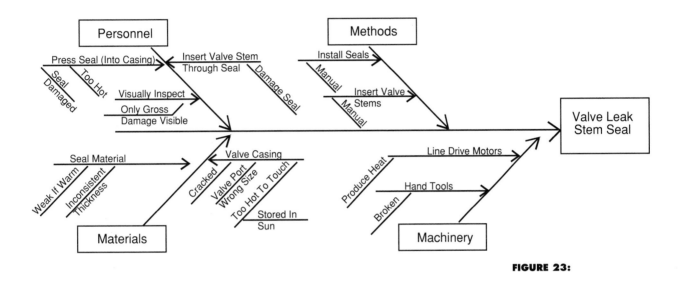

FIGURE 23:

POSSIBLE SOLUTIONS

Once the diagram was completed, a designer noted the frequency with which the issue of temperature arose. He told the group that the particular valve stem sealing material they used has excellent resistance to smooth friction at virtually all use temperatures, but that it was prone to tear if stretched at temperatures above 85 degrees Fahrenheit. Further evaluation of the fishbone revealed the fact that there were potentially controllable heat sources in their assembly process. As a matter of fact, reducing the temperature of the workplace and materials would also improve employee comfort.

Once some relatively simple and inexpensive steps were taken to improve heat ventilation in the work area and provide for a cooler valve body storage facility, the incidence of returned or rejected valves dropped significantly.

The fishbone diagram, when applied conscientiously, can be used to identify root causes that traditional problem-review processes would never identify.

Hints regarding the use of the fishbone diagram:

1. There are slight variations in the construction of the fishbone. The variations primarily involve different methods by which you would identify classifications for your chart. Be open minded and flexible. If you have any difficulty identifying categories, fall back on the standard manufacturing and administrative classifications. You may be surprised how effectively those category titles can be applied to your needs.

2. Be certain that everyone in your group or team agrees on the problem you need to address (the box at the far right of your diagram). It would be extremely difficult to get honest, dedicated commitment from team members if they don't agree about *what* the problem is.

3. Don't allow your intuition about the cause of a problem to close your mind to an objective evaluation of other factors. As in the valve manufacturing example, the real problem may very well be something you'd never have considered without objectively reviewing all the data, and allowing for everyone's input.

THE RUN CHART

■ ■ ■ ■ ■ ■

There are no human-developed processes that are absolutely constant. No matter how carefully a process is planned and carried out, there will always be some amount of variation. While we may not be able to eradicate variance, we can (and should) monitor it. That's the purpose of the run chart; a tool developed to visually display the variations in a process.

As the sample run chart (Figure 24) illustrates, most applications of this tool involve the plotting of process data over a period of time. The process data may be:

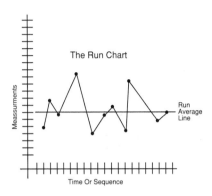

FIGURE 24:

• The number of units produced per hour in a manufacturing process,

• The quantity of a particular drug administered in a hospital by day of the week, by shift, etc.,

• The number of student absences by month,

• The hours of overtime per pay period,

• The number of customer purchases, complaints, inquiries per hour, etc.

In addition to the data points and the line connecting them, the run chart also displays a straight line representing the average of the data points on the chart. Once the data points are averaged, and the average is plotted on the chart, the user is able to see how much each data point varies from the average.

A run chart may be used to display data that occurs outside of your control (numbers of walk-in customers, numbers of patient appointment cancellations, etc.), or data that represents process activity over which you do potentially have some control (number of rejected machine parts, number of life insurance policies canceled due to billing problems, etc.).

Documenting the variation which you can adjust in a process is a logical action by almost anyone's standard. A large variation or series of variations may illustrate a need to adjust machinery or procedures.

The idea of applying a run chart to display variations outside your control may, at first glance, seem useless. There are, however, potential benefits from the illustration of these types of data as well. A consistent variation in the number of customers, for example, may help a store owner prepare a more effective personnel work schedule. There are probably dozens, if not hundreds, of potential applications of the run chart in every business.

TRAFFIC COURT "NO SHOWS"

Let's look at municipal traffic court's records relating to people who fail to appear for their citation hearings. This particular court is in session for traffic-related hearings three days each week, year around. The judge, concerned about the increasing number of "no-shows," asks the court staff to prepare a run chart to illustrate the "no-shows" by month of the year.

The staff reviews the court records for the most recent complete calendar year, and compiles the following data (Figure 25).

MONTH	NO SHOWS
JAN	8
FEB	14
MAR	11
APR	19
MAY	22
JUN	42
JUL	28
AUG	25
SEP	16
OCT	18
NOV	10
DEC	12

FIGURE 25:

With the data compiled, the staff are ready to create their run chart. In addition, the run average can be calculated and added to the chart.

The average is calculated by adding together all of the monthly totals (213 total "no shows"), and dividing by the number of data points (12). The run average for the chart will be 17.75.

The run chart, as you recall from the sample on the first page of this section, displays the time or sequence (months, in this illustration) along the bottom, and the measurements (number of "no shows") on the left side. The left-side data numbers must extend to at least 42, the largest number of monthly "no shows."

The staff prepares the chart and plots the data points (monthly "no show" totals), then connects the months consecutively to create a visual representation of last year's "no shows" (Figure 26).

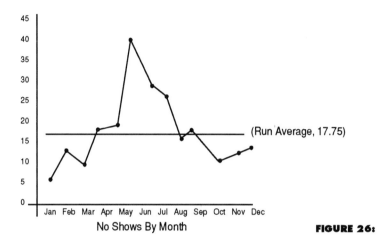

No Shows By Month   **FIGURE 26:**

As is the case with all the quality tools, there are some basics relating to this tool's construction and interpretation. In the case of the run chart, be aware of the following interpretation and evaluation standards:

•   The left/vertical side of the chart is referred to as the y axis (see Figure 27).

•   The bottom/horizontal side of the chart is referred to as the x axis (see Figure 27).

•   The x axis should be expressed in terms of time (hours, days, months, etc.) or other sequence (work shift, batch, etc.). The y axis should indicate the number of units needed to incorporate all the points of data (see Figure 27).

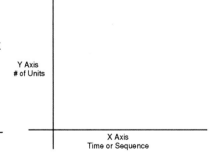

FIGURE 27:

•   Keep the data organized in the same chronological order in which it was recorded.

•   When interpreting the data displayed on a run chart, remember that variation is a natural part of any repeated process. Don't jump to conclusions or make changes in the process each time the process changes. Look for significant variations which might be caused by unique, preventable causes.

• A chart that portrays a very "tight" grouping of data points around the average line may be in excellent control, or you may have made the range of measurements too large (Figure 28, A). Try to construct the y axis so the largest and smallest data points fall relatively near the top and bottom of the chart, respectively.

• If a significant number of data points (e.g., more than half the number of all data points plotted) fall consecutively on one side of the average, your process may merit investigation (Figure 28, B).

• If a process is plotted over an extended period of time, and the chart illustrates sudden, but apparently permanent change in the average, investigate your process for causes of the change. You'll want to eliminate the negative causes and standardize the positive ones.

The traffic court run chart (Figure 26) displayed a significant variation in "no shows" in June. In looking for causes, the judge and her staff noted that most of the "no shows" in June were college age people who, probably, simply decided not to return following graduation or dropping out of the local university. A number of potential remedies might be considered and employed to reduce that number.

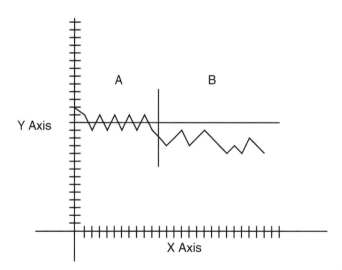

FIGURE 28:

THE BARBELL CHART (HISTOGRAM)

A natural part of any repeated process is "variation." No matter how closely one follows standardized steps or procedures, the product of those efforts will always vary to some degree. You've no doubt experienced this phenomenon, whether it was a quality problem with a particular supplier's parts, or the unpredictable texture of a batch of home made chocolate chip cookies.

Most if not every process will produce a few products that are perfect, a significant amount of acceptable products, and a few that are too flawed to be of use. The basic objective of anyone who repeatedly performs a process should be to reduce the overall variation in that process and to maximize the number of perfect or near perfect products. The first step in reducing the variation in a process is to accurately measure and illustrate the amount of variation that already exists in that process. The **BARBELL CHART** is a tool specifically designed to accomplish just that. By following a few simple steps, anyone can learn to prepare a barbell chart to illustrate the variation in virtually any process from which you can capture basic measurement data. Figure 29 is a barbell chart displaying distribution of adult males by height.

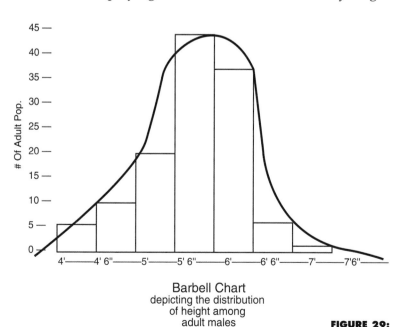

Barbell Chart
depicting the distribution
of height among
adult males

FIGURE 29:

A barbell can also be used to provide a clear visual representation of natural distributions (e.g., the height of 8th grade students, how long it takes for people to cross a street, etc.). Most natural distributions, as well as most repeated manufacturing processes will produce variations that, when charted on a **BAR** graph, will form a somewhat **BELL**-shaped curve (though most distributions don't form perfect bell shapes), hence, the title **BARBELL CHART**. For those who have a statistical background, or who have a more formalized TQM background, the barbell may be recognized by its more traditional TQM title, the **HISTOGRAM**.

A barbell chart can be constructed to illustrate the variation in any process, assuming you can capture some very basic kinds of data. In essence, you need to determine:

1. The number of pieces of datum (e.g., how many widgets, how many 8th grade students, etc.)

2. A consistent unit of measurement (e.g., millimeters of thickness, inches of height, etc.)

3. A consistent means of applying the measurement to the data (e.g., widgets are measured with a calibrated micrometer, all students are measured in bare feet, etc.)

Since these minimum elements of data collection can be met in relation to most things we do, the only concern at this point is... how does one construct a barbell chart?

CHARTING STUDENT SPRINT TIMES

A high school physical education teacher, Susan Gale, wanted to determine the distribution of students' times in the 100 meter dash. The appropriate tool for that purpose is, of course, the barbell chart. Susan already has all of her students' 100 meter times recorded in her grade book. She records the times on a single piece of paper. The raw data sheet looks like this:

14.3	15.3	13.2	16.8	16.6	13.8	14.4
17.2	17.0	16.7	17.7	17.0	14.4	14.9
13.6	19.2	17.0	14.4	14.7	15.3	15.3
12.0	13.9	13.9	15.2	15.0	15.0	14.9
17.3	11.9	14.5	14.9	14.8	14.8	15.7
15.5	15.1	15.3	15.4	16.0	15.7	15.9
18.0	16.3	14.9	15.3	16.2	16.1	16.4
16.2	17.0	16.2	14.8	14.0	15.0	15.9
16.6	17.2	15.9	15.3	16.5	15.3	14.8
15.3	14.8	15.5	14.2	17.1	14.9	15.3

In order to prepare the time data for illustration on a barbell chart, Susan follows a series of standardized steps.

1. She first **COUNTS THE NUMBER OF PIECES OF INDIVIDUAL DATUM.** In this case the number is 70.

2. The next step is to **DETERMINE THE RANGE OF THE DATA**. The range is simply the difference between the largest and the smallest data points. In Susan's data, the range is determined by subtracting the fastest time (11.9 seconds) from the slowest time (19.2 seconds). Susan's data range, therefore, is 7.3 seconds.

3. The third step involves **SELECTING A SPECIFIC NUMBER OF DATA CLASSES**. A data class is a span of data (times, thicknesses, etc.) that will be included in a single bar. Each data class will become a bar on the finished chart, so you need to determine how many you would like to display. The number of bars on most barbell charts is traditionally between 5 and 20. In some manufacturing processes there are thousands of individual data points, and a barbell chart used to illustrate the variation in a process might have 20 or even more classes, or chart bars. In this case, it would be more appropriate to select from 6-10 classes; let's say 8. This decision is more subjective than absolute, so don't worry that you may select the "wrong" number of classes for your own use. The following table provides an approximate guideline for selecting an appropriate number of classes:

Number of Data Points	Number of Classes
Under 50	5-7
50-100	6-10
100-250	7-12
over 250	10-20

FIGURE 30:

4. With the range and number of data classes determined, Susan will **CALCULATE THE CLASS WIDTH**, or the span of data measurement that will be represented by each bar (in Susan's case, time). In order to calculate the class width, all Susan has to do is divide the range (7.3 seconds) by the number of classes or bars (8). The quotient of this calculation is .9125 seconds per class or bar. Since Susan's original data is documented only to tenths of a second, she will round her class width to the closest tenth, in this case, her rounded class width is .90.

5. At this point, Susan will **CALCULATE THE CLASS BOUNDARIES** for each class or bar (the slowest and fastest times that will be represented by each bar). She starts with the fastest time of 11.9 seconds, and uses that as the fastest time to be represented in the first bar. She will then add the class width (.90) to 11.9 to determine the fastest time that would be represented by the second bar, then add .90 to that number to determine the fastest time to be represented by the third bar, and so on. Once all Susan's calculations are completed, she will have eight equal divisions of time. Her basic chart, minus the bars, can now be constructed as follows (Figure 31).

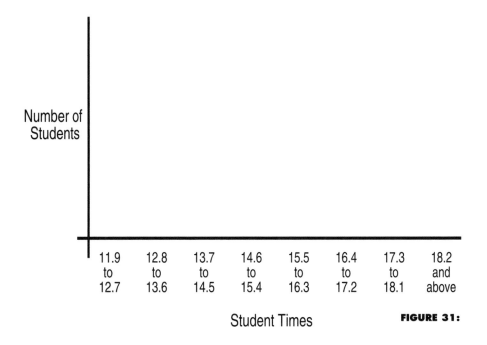

FIGURE 31:

Note that the slowest boundary time for each bar goes to, but does not include, the starting boundary time for the next class. Since Susan rounded her original class width from .9125 to .90, she will have one time that exceeds the last bar boundary. Susan chooses to include that slowest time in the final class.

6. Susan now retrieves the paper with all of the students' times and tabulates them on a check sheet, using the same class boundaries as she will employ on her barbell chart. Her completed check sheet looks like Figure 32.

11.9-12.7   11

12.8-13.6   1111

13.7-14.5   1̶1̶1̶1̶   1̶1̶1̶1̶

14.6-15.4   1̶1̶1̶1̶   1̶1̶1̶1̶   1̶1̶1̶1̶   1̶1̶1̶1̶   111

15.5-16.3   1̶1̶1̶1̶   1̶1̶1̶1̶   1̶1̶1̶1̶

16.4-17.2   1̶1̶1̶1̶   1̶1̶1̶1̶   11

17.3-18.1   111

18.2-...   1

FIGURE 32:

7. The final step for Susan to do simply involves drawing the bars on her prepared chart. The vertical axis (number of students) can now be established, in that she knows that the greatest number of data points in any one class is 23. Susan's final barbell chart looks like this:

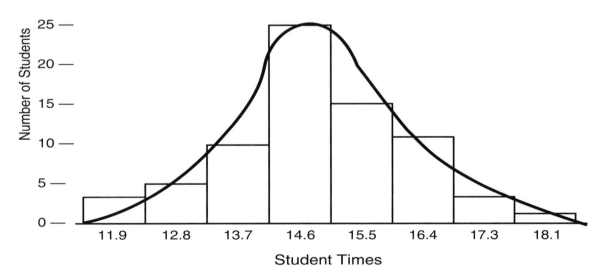

FIGURE 33:

Should Susan want to compare the distribution of this year's students' times with the times of future groups, she would maintain the same class boundaries and vertical axis values, and plot the next year's data points (100 meter times) on the graph. A quick comparison of various years' charts could easily identify trends in student speed.

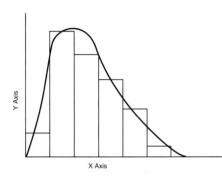

FIGURE 34A:

The traditional application of the barbell chart is in the manufacturing field, and it is a tool that is in constant use by organizations applying statistical quality control. As in our illustration, however, the barbell chart can be applied to any of a wide variety of situations.

When evaluating data illustrated via barbell charts, look for variations in the standard bell shape. While some processes may be naturally skewed high or low (the top of the bell is much closer to one side (Figure 34A)), be especially aware of any process that displays an unusual bell shape. A wide, low bell shape may indicate that your process is producing too few units of optimum quality and too many mediocre ones (Figure 34B). A double-humped bell (Figure 34C) may indicate a wide variation in quality in units produced by different shifts or work groups. (In that case, try constructing a different chart for each group or shift.) A process that produces a significantly different bell each time the process is evaluated may indicate a problem in the quality of that process *or* a variation in the accuracy of your measurement methods. The more you use this, and all your QC Tools, the greater benefit you will realize from the data you produce every day.

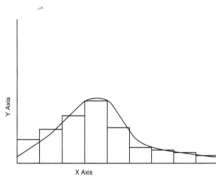

FIGURE 34B:

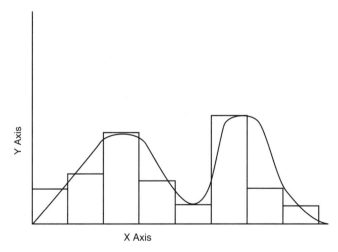

FIGURE 34C:

THE SCATTER DIAGRAM

■ ■ ■ ■ ■ ■

Many things in life have an assumed "cause and effect" relationship. All other factors equal, if we increase our calorie intake, our weight will increase. If you receive commission on sales, a decrease in sales will result in a decrease in your income.

There are other, less obvious pairs of factors, however, which may or may not have interrelationships. Since controlling the consistency of a process is valuable, it would be helpful to determine which variables may affect changes in that process. The scatter diagram is a tool specifically designed to allow you to investigate and display the presence or lack of correlation between two variables. It will allow you to visually determine whether an increase in one variable consistently correlates with an increase or decrease in the other variable.

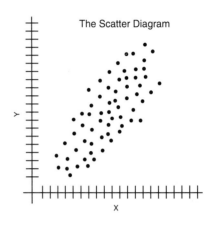

The Scatter Diagram

FIGURE 35:

ART GALLERY SALES

An art gallery owner overheard his sales person express an opinion that people who visited the gallery in the early part of the day were "small buyers," while those who visited near the end of the day were "big buyers." The two discussed the sales person's observations and decided that, if the assertion were correct, it would be helpful in determining more effective opening and closing hours.

Over the next month, all sales receipts were marked with the time that the sale was made. At the end of the month, the owner took the time of day information and the dollar amount of the purchase from the 72 sales receipts and prepared a scatter diagram. The two variables (time of sale, and dollar amount of sales) will be plotted on the scatter diagram.

The variable under investigation (time of day in this illustration) should be placed on the bottom of the chart (the x axis), and the other variable (dollars in sales) will be plotted on the left side of the diagram (the y axis).

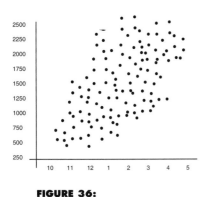

FIGURE 36:

The maximum individual sale amount was $2500, while the smallest amount was $275. The y axis will be marked to accommodate those upper and lower points. The gallery is open from 10:00 a.m. until 5:00 p.m., so the hours from 10:00 to 5:00 will be identified across the x axis on the bottom of the diagram.

The gallery owner prepares the diagram, and plots all 72 sales on the chart by placing a dot above the time of the purchase, at the appropriate height for the dollar amount of the sale. Once all the sales were plotted, the completed scatter diagram looked like Figure 36.

INTERPRETING A SCATTER DIAGRAM

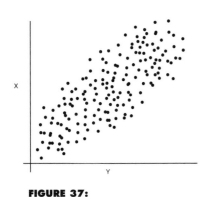

FIGURE 37:

The interpretation of a scatter diagram is somewhat subjective. A visual evaluation is made regarding the general pattern of the dots. If the pattern looks like Figure 37 you can be fairly certain that there is a "positive correlation" between the two factors, that is, when x increases, y usually increases as well. It generally is cautioned that you not automatically interpret that to mean that x "causes" y. Since there are possibly other, unrecognized factors affecting y, you can only determine, at this point, that there is an apparent positive correlation between x and y.

A somewhat looser, but similar pattern, like our illustrated example (Figure 36), can reasonably be interpreted as indicating a "possible" positive correlation between x and y. This possible positive correlation indicates that an increase in x may result in an increase in y. Other scatter chart patterns and their meanings are represented in Figures 38-41.

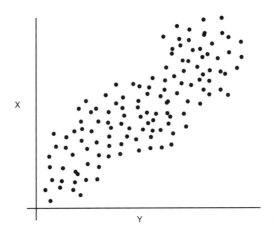

FIGURE 38:

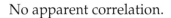
No apparent correlation.

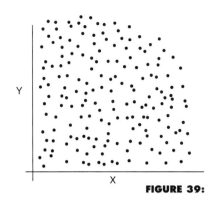

FIGURE 39:

Possible "negative correlation,"
as x increases, y may decrease.

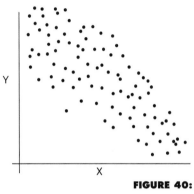

FIGURE 40:

Negative correlation.
An increase in x usually
results in a decrease in y.

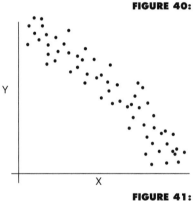

FIGURE 41:

        Scatter diagrams that might display a negative correlation,
for example, may be those displaying prevention actions. One
would expect to see the pattern above (Figure 41) in a chart representing frequency of brushing one's teeth on the x axis, and the
number of dental cavities on the y axis. As the frequency of brushing increases, the number of cavities will probably decrease.

Looking back at the scatter diagram produced by the art gallery owner (Figure 36), we can see that there is a pattern which we would probably describe as a possible positive correlation between the time of day and the dollar amount of sales. While, with the correlation displayed, the owner may not be justified in making drastic changes in his scheduling, he certainly has identified a marketing variable which deserves continued monitoring.

Use the scatter diagram any time you want to investigate the presence or lack of interrelationship between two variables. Your efforts may very well result in surprising benefits.

THE CONTROL CHART

■ ■ ■ ■ ■ ■

S ince variation is a natural part of any repeated process, it's inappropriate and wasteful to modify a process every time it results in a measurably different product. On the other hand, it's fiscal suicide to allow a process to develop excessive, potentially controllable levels of variation. The solution, of course, is to monitor all processes and modify them only when there is too much change.

That, in essence, is the purpose of the control chart. In a preceding section of this text, you were introduced to a tool referred to as a run chart. The run chart is a tool which allows you to document the changes in a process over a period of time (see pages 37-40). The control chart is nothing more than a run chart with statistically calculated lines added to illustrate the process upper and, when appropriate, lower boundaries of anticipated variation.

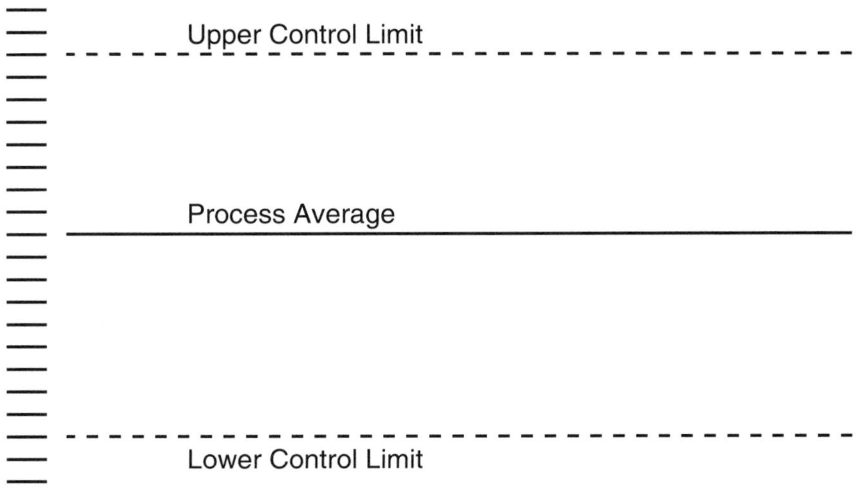

Upper Control Limit

Process Average

Lower Control Limit

FIGURE 42:

The objective of some processes may be to consistently produce above the upper control limit (e.g., sales per month). Service providers may desire to regularly provide a service sooner or more quickly than the calculated lower control limit. A hospital emergency room staff, of course, would like to provide medical evaluations immediately upon patient arrival, though a data calculated control chart would still have a lower control limit. While E.R. staff might like to set a lower control limit of zero, they will learn that control limits must be the result of statistical calculation, not simply desirable standards.

A more traditional control chart is one documenting a dimension of a manufactured item for which there are known specifications. A particular item may be too thick (or heavy, rough, etc.) and be rejected. The same item may be too thin (or light, slick, etc.) and also be rejected. A control chart employed to monitor the performance of the process which produces that item would appropriately display an upper and lower control limit line.

An important concept to understand at this point is that a control chart will allow us to monitor a process and calculate the process' upper and lower control limits. Those limits may or may not fall within the specification limits established for the item being produced. In other words, you may have a process with a capacity to produce items of four millimeters thickness deviation from the ideal. If your customer will only accept items with two millimeters or less deviation, your process can be running in control and still produce a very high percentage of "defective" items. Such a process is, of course, in need of significant modification, if the organization hopes to be profitable.

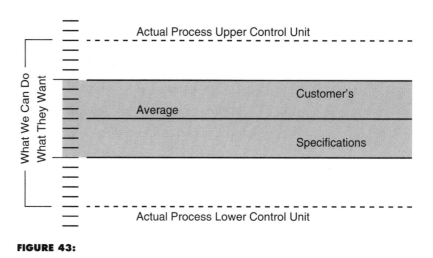

FIGURE 43:

The upper and lower controls are calculated after a series of sample products from a process have been taken. For the limits to be meaningful, the samples must be taken while the process is functioning "normally," or without any customized or temporary adjustments. If a process evaluation is to be of any real value it must be completed honestly and objectively. Adjusting a process, even slightly during the data-gathering phase may make your process "look" better, but such adjustments can make truly effective change much more difficult to institute.

The "normal" operation of the process to be evaluated should include the necessary and regular activities which affect the process (e.g., regular maintenance, standard work shift/ overtime schedules, raw material quality, etc.). Don't intentionally modify your process during the period of time in which you select your samples.

Unique or special factors (e.g., unusual mechanical malfunctions, atypical raw material problems, or significant employee error, etc.) will improperly affect the sample products taken from the process. All unique or special factors should be identified and brought under control before a truly normal group of samples can be taken.

PENS-R-US CONTROL CHART

Brian Wirth is founder and president of Pens-R-Us, a relatively small ball point pen manufacturer. He began to receive an increasing number of returned pens, indicating the customer's dissatisfaction with the quality of the pens. Brian had his secretary compile a list of the specific complaints. He categorized the complaints and charted them on a descending bar chart. The chart clearly indicated that the vast majority of the complaints were in reference to pens that came apart at the threaded divider in the pen body. With only slight force, many pens pulled apart at the threads. Once a defective pen was pulled apart, it could not be securely threaded together again.

Brian called the plastic injection mold supervisor and scheduled a meeting. The supervisor, Tammi Simmons, responded to Brian's inquiries with interest. The two constructed a fishbone diagram to investigate the possible sources of the faulty thread problem. Tammi identified several probable causal factors relating to the plastic injection molds themselves, the grade of plastic used, and the procedure of removing the completed pen bodies from the molds. As they continued with their fishbone diagram, the plastic injection process began to appear to be the most probable source of problems.

Brian inquired about the actual thread-making capabilities of the machinery Tammi's division was utilizing. She indicated that the injectors had been used previously on another line without problems. The other line, however, produced a non-retracting pen body which had no threads. Because Pens-R-Us had begun producing threaded body pens only eight months earlier, they had an insufficient amount of prior, relevant data available relating to this specific issue.

Tammi recommended that a series of samples be taken from the line and carefully evaluated. The thread depth, she indicated, should be carefully measured on both pen body sections. The resulting data could then be utilized to construct a control chart which would thereby identify the thread-making capacity of the current process. Brian suggested a few alterations which might make the process somewhat more effective, but agreed with Tammi's recommendation that the process capabilities be evaluated initially without any modifications, especially since the modifications suggested might or might not improve the product.

Tammi decided to establish a consistent format for sampling the pen barrel injection line. She decided to consistently take one out of every ten pen barrels. Tammi returned to the plastic injection line and, at the top of the hour, began to retrieve every tenth pen barrel ejected from the molds. She continued the procedure for one minute every other hour of the work day, securing a total of eight pen barrels from each semi-hourly sampling. By the end of the work day, she had set aside each of the sample sets, labeled for the hour of selection, and placed in the exact order in which she had chosen them. Tammi continued this procedure for an entire work week. She then delivered the pen barrels to the plant technical supervisor and requested that each barrel be inspected, specifically relating to the thread depth.

The technical supervisor, familiar with the quality control tools, was able to apply the data supplied by Tammi to a control chart. Because the data he would be working with were exclusively physical measurement, the technical supervisor appropriately selected an $\overline{X}$-R (X Bar R, or Average and Range) control chart. The $\overline{X}$-R control chart is used any time the data is expressed in specific units of measurement (e.g., depth, weight, units of time, etc.). His initial efforts involved coordinating Tammi's data into a simple table. With the necessary data easily available in this format, the technical supervisor is able to construct a control chart for thread depth on Tammi's plastic mold line. The data from one day's samples are listed below:

FIGURE 44:

Monday January 20

Time Of Sample	# In Sample (Set)	Thread Depths (In mm.)
0900 Hrs	8	0.52, 0.44, 0.38, 0.48 0.55, 0.41, 0.40. 0.49
1100 Hrs	8	0.36, 0.44, 0.46, 0.55 0.46, 0.51, 0.52, 0.48
1300 Hrs	8	0.40, 0.48, 0.52, 0.33 0.49, 0.51, 0.46, 0.48
1500 Hrs	8	0.48, 0.39, 0.47, 0.50 0.44, 0.48, 0.42, 0.51
1700 Hrs	8	0.42, 0.48, 0.41, 0.47 0.44, 0.49, 0.43, 0.49

With the data listed, the technical supervisor is able to prepare a control chart by plugging the above data into a relatively simple set of equations. The resulting numerical data will establish:

A. An overall average of thread depth for Tammi's plastic mold line,

B. An "Upper Control Limit," or maximum thread depth produced by Tammi's mold line when the line is functioning normally,

C. A "Lower Control Limit," or minimum thread depth produced by the same line under the same normal conditions,

D. A process range (difference between the largest and smallest measurement in each set), which is generally plotted on a separate range chart which accompanies the control chart.

The first calculation the technical supervisor performs involves computing the average thread depth of each set (semi-hourly sample group). As an example, the first set on Monday (9:00 a.m.) has eight samples: 0.52, 0.44, 0.38, 0.48, 0.55, 0.41, 0.40 and 0.49. The average is computed by adding all of the sample measurements and dividing that sum by the number of measurements in the set (8). The technical supervisor calculates the 9:00 a.m. average by adding:

Add Samples:

	0.52
	0.44
	0.38
	0.48
	0.55
	0.41
	0.40
+	0.49
	3.67

$0.52 + 0.44 + 0.38 + 0.48 + 0.55 + 0.41 + 0.40 + 0.49 = 3.67$; then by dividing 3.67 by 8, the number of samples. The average thread depth measurement for the first set, therefore, is 0.4588

The set range is simply the difference between the largest and smallest measurement in the set (0.52 - 0.38 = 0.14)

Divide Total by Number of Samples:
$3.67 \div 8 = 0.4588$

Tammi collected a total of 25 sets of data (five per day for five days). Each set is averaged in the same manner as the first set. The set averages for the week are listed on this page (Figure 46).

Set #	Set Average (Thread Depth)	Set Range
1	0.4588	0.14
2	0.4725	0.19
3	0.4588	0.19
4	0.4613	0.12
5	0.4538	0.08
6	0.4767	0.11
7	0.4667	0.08
8	0.4333	0.07
9	0.4825	0.09
10	0.4795	0.12
11	0.4550	0.08
12	0.4300	0.15
13	0.4450	0.08
14	0.4225	0.13
15	0.4280	0.09
16	0.4775	0.05
17	0.4905	0.12
18	0.4676	0.11
19	0.4350	0.07
20	0.4650	0.12
21	0.4525	0.13
22	0.4875	0.10
23	0.4495	0.08
24	0.4750	0.11
25	0.4666	0.08

FIGURE 46:

Note that the set average is calculated to two decimal points more than the measurements, a standard for the application of the set average.

With the data from this chart, the technical supervisor calculates the overall **PROCESS AVERAGE** by adding all 25 set averages and dividing that sum by the number of set averages (25). The sum of all of the set averages is 11.4911 which, when divided by 25, reveals a process average of 0.4596.

The **AVERAGE RANGE** is calculated similarly by adding all the set ranges and dividing by the total number of sets (25). The sum of all 25 set averages is 2.69. Once divided by 25, the average range for Tammi's data is determined to be .1076.

The only additional data needed to complete the calculations of the upper and lower control limits are provided on the following table (Figure 47). The values in this table are not a result of computations with the numbers in this example, but are consistent for any data applied to an average and range control chart. By selecting the proper numerical factor from the table, based on the number of individual samples in each set (8 in this example), the technical supervisor has all the necessary data to complete his calculation of control limits for Tammi's plastic mold process.

Table of Factors for $\overline{X}$ & R Charts			
Number of observations in subgroup (n)	Factors for X Chart	Factors for R Chart	
	A_1	Lower D_3	Upper D_4
2	1.880	0	3.268
3	1.023	0	2.574
4	0.729	0	2.282
5	0.577	0	2.114
6	0.483	0	2.004
7	0.419	0.076	1.924
8	0.373	0.136	1.864
9	0.337	0.184	1.816
10	0.308	0.223	1.777

FIGURE 47:

The technical supervisor prepares to calculate the upper control limit for the process average chart by selecting the A2 value of 0.373 (for 8 units per sample). He uses that A2 value 0.373 in the following equation:

Upper Control Limit (UCL) = Process Average $(\overline{X})$ + (A2 x Average Range (R))

By inserting the values earlier calculated for the process average and the average range, as well as the A2 value (0.373) from the chart, the equation becomes:

UCL = .4596 + (0.373 x .1076)
UCL = .4596 + 0.0413
UCL = .5009

The lower control limit (LCL) can also be calculated by inserting the same values into the following equation:

Lower Control Limit = Process Average $(\overline{X})$ — (A2 x Average Range (R))

LCL = .4596 — (0.373 x .1076)
LCL = .4596 — (0.0401)
LCL = .4195

With the process average, the upper control limit, and the lower control limit known, the process' control chart can be constructed. The traditional control chart will display the process average in the middle of the chart as a heavy, solid line. The upper and lower control limits are plotted as dotted or broken lines above and below the process average line.

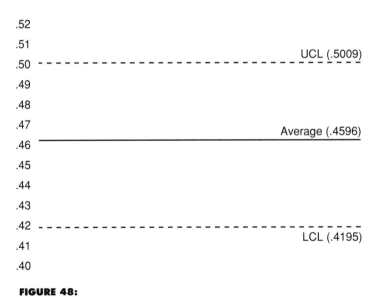

FIGURE 48:

With the newly constructed control chart in hand, the technical supervisor makes a trip to Tammi's plastic mold line. He instructs her to continue to take periodic sets of samples from her line. Once she delivers the samples to the technical supervisor, he will measure the thread depths and plot the data on the control chart, then send the plotted chart back to Tammi. She can then use the chart to determine whether her line is producing thread quality within the processes' calculated control limits, or whether there are trends reflected on the chart which might indicate a need to investigate the process.

There are a variety of trends on a control chart that deserve further evaluation. The traditional control chart trends which merit an investigation of the process include:

A. Any point that falls above the upper control limit line or below the lower control limit line (1),

B. A small group of points (two out of three) that is nearly at the upper or lower control limit lines (2a),

C. A moderate sized group (four out of five) that falls near the center of either the upper or lower control areas (2b),

D. A large number (nine or more) of consecutive points that falls on the same side of the average line (2c),

E. A significant number of points (six or more in a row) that continues to increase or decrease (2d),

F. A large number of points (fourteen or more) that either alternates up and down, or falls close to, and on the same side of the centerline (2e and 2f).

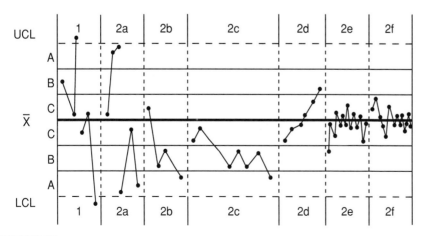

FIGURE 49:

There is a high probability that the listed variations are the result of something that can be controlled. Any charted process that displays one or more of the listed variations is considered to be "**OUT OF CONTROL**." Every out-of-control process should be further investigated to determine what factor(s) may have affected the process. Any process that consistently produces samples that fall between the upper and lower control limits is considered to be "**IN CONTROL**."

In Tammi's case, she now has a clear picture of the thread-making capacity of her plastic mold line. Should the technical division determine, however, that the minimum thread depth for a secure hold is over .4596 (the process average), Tammi can confidently report that the process, as it now exists, is not consistently producing products that meet those standards. Assuming that Tammi's production line is not currently producing threads of adequate dimension, carefully calculated adjustments can be initiated. Had Brian initially demanded an uncontrolled trial and error method of process adjustment, the inherent inadequacy of the process would not have been identified until much later, if ever.

Many processes can be modified so as to increase their efficiency, but it is highly unlikely that the correct changes will be identified and implemented without a careful evaluation of the initial capacity of the system.

The process average control chart will be accompanied with a **RANGE CONTROL CHART**. This chart displays the variations in ranges of each set, and can be helpful in determining if fluctuation in the process average is a result of a few units that vary greatly, or a full set of units that consistently vary from the process average.

The range control chart calculations use values from the previous Table of Factors (Figure 47), in addition to the calculated average range (.1076 in our example above). The control limit equations for the range control chart (for an $\overline{X}$-R) are:

Upper Range Control Limit = D4 (from the table, Figure 47) x Average Range

When we apply the data from our example, we plug-in the following data:

UCL (range) = 1.864 x .1076
**   UCL(r) = .2006**

The lower range control limit is determined with the following equation:

Lower Range Control Limit = D3 (from the table Figure 47) x Average Range

With our sample data, the equation becomes:

LCL (range) = 0.136 x .1076
**   LCL(r) = 0.0146**

    The range control chart for our example can be constructed as follows:

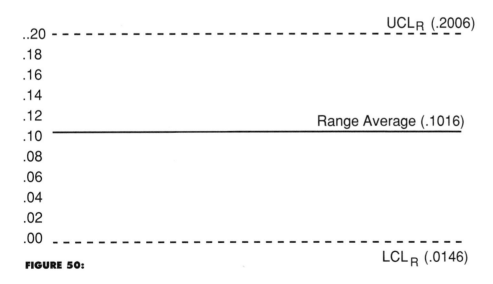

FIGURE 50:

Using our statistically prepared X̄-R control charts, we can plot data from the process to determine whether the process is *"in"* or *"out"* of control. We can also visually evaluate the ranges in the data of each set. If we take the data from the samples that Tammi secured on Monday, January 20 (Figure 44), our process control chart and accompanying range control chart look like this:

Process Control Chart

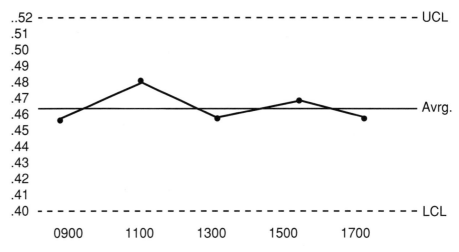

FIGURE 51:

Range Control Chart

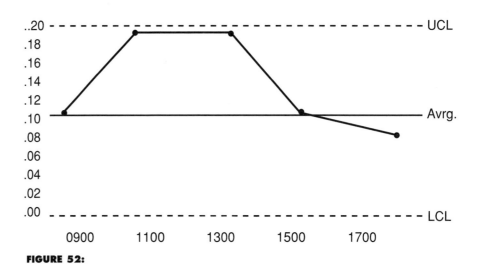

FIGURE 52:

This combination of charts is an illustration of the benefit of considering both the process average and the process range. As you can see, the process control chart indicates a process running very close to the established average, generally a favorable indicator. The range chart, however, displays two successive points very near the upper control limit. This lack of consistency indicates that the average of each semi-hourly set is made up of individual data points which vary widely. If this pattern were to continue, it would be obvious that this process allows for significant and consistent variation, in spite of the excellent average documented in the process control chart. Remedial action may be merited, depending on further analysis of the process.

Assuming the process is producing items that meet minimum standards, care should be taken to at least maintain the process. If significant deviations occur, remedial action may be required. As part of your inquiry into possible causes of an "out-of-control" process, you might want to consider the following possible factors:

A. Change in instruments used to measure products,

B. Personnel variations (operator training level, fatigue, shift, or line assignment, etc.),

C. Variations in raw materials used (change in suppliers, etc.),

D. Variations in environment (temperature, humidity, light, etc.),

E. Machinery (wear, maintenance, adjustments, etc.).

The control chart is a tool of immense value, but has limited application for many businesses. The number of sample sets for the $\overline{X}$-R control chart, for example, should be about 20-25. As you have seen in the table of factors, the recommended number of units per set is between 2 and 10. This indicates that a process must produce a sufficient number of products to allow a sampling of a minimum of 40 units (20 sets of 2). It is frequently recommended, in fact, that an $\overline{X}$-R control chart be based on a minimum of 100 data points. Many processes produce far too few products to merit application of this statistical tool. Attempting to construct certain types of control charts with a significantly smaller number of data points may be counter-productive, since a single data point may unreasonably sway the calculations in a small statistical sample.

Keep in mind that a control chart that documents change in a favorable direction equally, merits investigation. Only by determining what caused "good" change can you hope to regularly recreate that improvement.

The control chart example used in this section is known as an average and range control chart. Other types of control charts have been formulated to chart processes by the number of rejected units produced and by the number of specific defects found in samples. Other types of control charts are employed when sampling a process for qualitative characteristics (e.g., acceptable/not acceptable, defective/not defective). Other types of control charts include:

- The p chart: for determining the proportion of defective units in a subgroup,

- The np chart: for calculating the number of defective units,

- The c chart: for calculating the number of nonconformities with a constant sample size,

- The L chart: for calculating the number of nonconformities with varying sample size.

Each type of control chart requires a unique set of calculations. While the control charts appear to be complicated tools that require specialized mathematical training, they can be applied by anyone who receives some basic instruction. There are calculators available which will make the necessary calculations, once the basic data is punched-in.

For more detailed information about control charts, read *The Memory Jogger*™, available through GOAL/QPC, or seek out books relating to "statistical process control" in your library.

TOOL BAG #2 THE SEVEN MANAGEMENT AND PLANNING TOOLS

I f you have read the preceding sections of this text, you learned about the Quality Control (QC) Tools. Those tools provided simple designs for the illustration and utilization of data. As the label for this second tool bag implies, the Management and Planning (MP) Tools afford the user a series of implements that help turn less specific information into precise, planned actions.

Unlike the QC Tools, the MP Tools provide a format for the quantification of ideas and "feelings." Identifying the needs of the customer, determining the most essential objectives for addressing those needs, and turning those essential objectives into specific work tasks are all attainable goals—not simply dreams. The MP Tools can provide your organization with the ability to accomplish all these objectives, and more!

As you proceed through the MP Tool descriptions, you'll probably identify applications in your own personal or professional activities. After perusing this text, take advantage of the first opportunity to apply them. You don't have to know everything about TQM before taking advantage of the benefit of its parts.

A business vignette is provided as an illustration for each tool. As you read and study, allow your mind to expand on the possible applications. The limit of usefulness of these tools is no greater than the limit of your own creative capacity.

The tools described in this section are:

1. **THE AFFINITY DIAGRAM** - A tool that provides you with a means of coordinating large numbers of different pieces of information into natural groupings.

2. **THE INTERRELATIONSHIP DIGRAPH** - A graphic means of determining the presence and strength of relationships among a number of issues, ideas, or activities.

3. **THE TREE DIAGRAM** - A process of breaking major goals or objectives into specific actions.

4. **THE PRIORITIZATION MATRIX** - A clear and concise method for assigning relative values to different criteria, and a means of comparing a number of options to the same criteria.

5. **THE MATRICES** - A variety of applications of several different matrix diagram formats. Each allows the user to compare two, three, or even four sets of data to one another.

6. **THE PROCESS DECISION PROGRAM CHART (PDPC)** - A format for preparing alternative action steps during the planning of new, unique, or high stakes processes.

7. **THE ACTIVITY NETWORK** - A sophisticated time-line, which identifies the order of actions, as well as the earliest and latest start and finish times for each individual action.

THE AFFINITY DIAGRAM

The Affinity Diagram

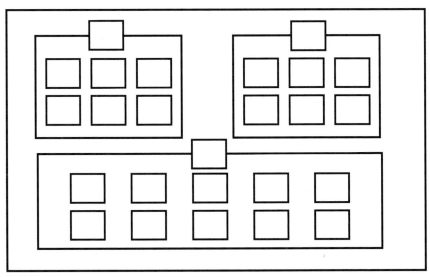

FIGURE 53:

"

A FFINITY: An inherent similarity between or among things."

The affinity diagram is a tool that allows a group (or sometimes an individual) to organize a large and diverse collection of concepts into natural groupings. You'll notice that the units to be grouped with the affinity diagram are no longer bits of statistical data, but "concepts." In keeping with that, the concepts are expressed as written language and not mathematical units.

The affinity diagram is one of the most diversely useful of the MP Tools. Once you are familiar with its application and flexibility, you will find it to be one of the most used implements in your tool box.

The traditional symbol used to represent the affinity diagram (above) is a clear representation of its format in use. While most working affinity diagrams are not as perfectly aligned as the symbol above, they do take on the same general appearance. As the logo represents, the affinity process begins with a large number of individual concepts written on small pieces of paper, and concludes with a smaller number of groupings of concepts with some natural similarity.

THE BAKER'S CRITICAL PROCESSES

Probably the most effective method of explaining the application of an affinity diagram is to provide a step-by-step illustration of a group affinity process.

In the TQM Overview section of this text the concept of "critical processes" was introduced. As you may recall, an individual's critical processes are those activities that the individual must perform in order to assure success in her/his endeavors. An individual may identify critical processes that are associated specifically with her/his professional activities, personal activities, or a combination. The total number of critical processes should be around 5, with a maximum of about 10. That section also advised that you could utilize the MP tool bag to identify your own critical processes. The affinity diagram is the specific tool that we'll use for that purpose.

No matter what your professional situation, whether CEO or factory worker, corporate magnate or small business owner, your personal and/or professional critical processes are identified in the same manner. To begin, ask yourself this simple question; "Who are my internal and external customers?"

If you are a small bakery owner, your list may include:

INTERNAL	**EXTERNAL**
Full time employees	Walk-in customers
Part time employees	Special order customers
Bookkeeper	Suppliers
	Bank (business loan)

With your customers identified, it's time for a second question; "What do my customers need and expect from me?"

At this point, the affinity process is implemented. This process is much more productive when a group of perspectives is available. Since our baker has only two full time employees, besides his family members, he chooses to invite both employees and his wife to assist with the process. He closes the bakery early, and all employees sit around a clean, stainless steel topped dough table in the kitchen. The owner hands each employee a pad of sticky-backed notes, and tapes up his list of customers.

Before initiating the affinity process, he instructs them about the basic rules:

1. There are no "right" or "wrong" answers, only different perspectives. (No criticizing allowed.)

2. Write only one item on each piece of note paper.

3. Write legibly.

4. Construct each "need" with a noun and verb to clearly communicate the need.

"Now," he begins, "put yourself inside the head of each of these customers and tell me what each of them wants from me. Don't identify the customer on the note, just the need."

The employees exchange uncertain glances for several seconds before beginning to write. Once they begin, however, the sticky pieces of paper begin to litter the table top. The notes include needs like good pay, health insurance, fresh pastry, healthy food options, legible receipts, timely payments on mortgage, easy access for unloading supplies. After about five minutes, the production of new stickies ceases. The owner asks each employee to look over all the stickies to see if the ones produced by the other group members spark any new and different ideas. The group spends several minutes looking over the notes. Several additional notes are produced and the group settles down, prepared for the next step in the process.

The owner gives instructions for the step to follow. "I want each person to stand in a place that allows you to see the notes. If you see two "needs" that seem, in your mind, to be associated in some way, pick one of them up and place it next to the other." He further explains that there are only a few basic rules for this step in the affinity process:

1. No talking is allowed. This assures that no single, dominant individual will control the grouping process.

2. You may move a note that another group member has placed. If you find that the note is being moved back and forth, write the same "need" on another note and place it in the alternate group.

3. Be open-minded and creative during this process. Don't, for example, simply group in one place all the "needs" which seemed to be associated with one customer. Look instead for some similarity between and among specific "need" notes. Often, several customers will have shared needs (an "affinity" of needs) that this process will identify.

As the group members mill about the dough table surveying the collection of nearly 100 sticky notes, similarities start to become visible. Hands fly as the individual notes slowly begin to take the form of larger sets. When the note moving finally stops, the group has reduced the many of individual customer needs to just six large groups.

"Good work!" the baker lauds the workers. "We're almost done with our affinity process. The next thing we need to do is produce a topic heading for each of the six groupings." The headings generated by the group included:

1. Provide Employee Support/Assistance.
2. Maintain Positive Customer Relations.
3. Establish Sound Fiscal Management Process.
4. Assure Proper Store Maintenance.
5. Maintain Productive Community Involvement.
6. Continue Planning for Future Business Success.

The bakery owner now has a list of six general "customer needs" which account for the vast majority of his professional efforts. The affinity process is complete, and has provided a framework through which the bakery owner has objectively confirmed his primary customer-related obligations. He has taken advantage of a TQM business' most valuable asset—its employees' brains.

With the product from the affinity, the owner will identify (by himself, with his family, or with the entire group) the processes that **MUST** operate efficiently for all six categories of customer needs to be met. Those processes become his "critical processes," which he listed as:

1. Provide effective employee selection and TQM training.
2. Maintain positive market analysis and projection process.
3. Establish sound community relations.
4. Assure proper resource management.
5. Maintain productive baking skills.

The value of these issues extends beyond the identification of critical processes (they may be used, for example, to illustrate a vision of the organization in its perfect state).

Our bakery owner now has an outline of the processes at which he must be successful to be a thriving baker. With this information he can evaluate the time he spends each day to determine whether he has moved himself, his family, and his employees closer to their life goals.

OTHER USES

The affinity process can be used in many other applications. It can be used in a manner, similar to the preceding illustration, **TO ESTABLISH A PERSONAL OR PROFESSIONAL MISSION OR VISION OR TO ESTABLISH A MEETING AGENDA**. The first order of business for a hastily called meeting, for example, might be to have every person in attendance prepare a set of sticky notes in reference to the issues that (s)he would like to address. The meeting attendees then conduct an affinity grouping to determine a listing of general agenda issues which will accommodate all the individual issues. The old process of going around the table to give each attendee time to address his/her concerns often results in addressing the same general issue (personnel scheduling, for example) again and again. Addressing the topic from a more general perspective allows everyone to express concerns about their own needs, while at the same time providing an opportunity to hear other's problems in the same topic area. **AN AFFINITY MAY ALSO BE USED TO ESTABLISH GROUP OR COMPANY OBJECTIVES** from a plethora of personal or divisional "wants."

You could even apply an affinity **TO COORDINATE YOUR LIST OF "THINGS TO DO"** for the weekend. By grouping the list of miscellaneous activities into affinity headings, you can better determine which requires distant travel in one direction, which can be accomplished without assistance, which requires you to dress up, or any of a number of other categories which will allow you to accomplish the greatest number of activities with the shortest travel distance or preparation time.

The affinity diagram can be employed anytime an individual or group has a large number of ideas or issues that need to be condensed into a smaller number of more general topics. As is the case with all the MP Tools, the affinity process can be modified or altered to help address your specific needs.

The following is a list of general instructions for applying the affinity diagram:

1. **ASSEMBLE A TEAM.** If your business is small, like our baker's, you may choose to utilize all of your employees. If you have greater personnel resources, you can choose a team of employees and/or managers who have direct knowledge about the issue to be addressed. Be sure to select team members who represent a variety of perspectives and beliefs.

2. **AGREE ON THE TOPIC TO BE ADDRESSED** (e.g., customer needs, what we want to accomplish next year, what we want to do on our California vacation, etc.).

3. **HAVE MATERIALS AVAILABLE** to document specific pieces of information. We recommend adhesive backed notes because they can be secured on a vertical or horizontal surface, and can be picked up and replaced repeatedly.

4. **SOLICIT EVERYONE'S IDEAS.** In our bakery illustration, the notes were produced without group interaction, but you may choose to take turns making suggestions or randomly offer suggestions aloud, while one individual writes them on sticky notes. The group discussion method allows for every member to benefit from the varied thought processes of all members. It is important to reinforce the "no right/wrong answers" rule. Ridicule or amusement expressed toward any individual idea could create an inhibiting environment for creativity. Remember, the affinity process is a creative activity. When we require ourselves and others to think in a limited, traditional manner, we reduce the probability of creative and innovative solutions.

5. Have each team member **SEEK NATURAL SIMILARITIES (AFFINITIES)** among the notes and move the similar notes together. Continue this grouping activity until the note-moving ceases. Notes that are repeatedly moved between

groupings may be reproduced verbatim. One may then be placed into each grouping. Allow the individuals to function independently, reminding them only to "go with their gut." Promote creative thought processes. Since many problem-solution groups or teams include both supervisors and subordinates, this step can become dominated by the more powerful persons. Set the ground rules clearly and early, so one individual or group doesn't dominate.

TQM trainer experience indicates that a vertical surface is most effective in promoting full group access to the notes, but utilize any acceptable work surface to which you have access.

6. Once the affinity movement of sticky-back notes has stopped, and the general groupings are established, **CREATE "HEADERS"** or general topic cards for each group of notes. These headers may represent a step toward the solution to your problem, by identifying a number of general issues toward which you can apply your energy.

There are several probable responses people have upon being confronted with such a list of major tasks:

1. Now I know where to apply my efforts.

2. I don't have enough time or energy to accomplish **ALL** of these!

3. What, specifically, must I (we) do to accomplish these things?

If your reaction is similar to the first response, congratulations! If, however, your response is one or both of the other reactions, you're still in luck! There are other MP Tools specifically designed to provide you with solutions to your dilemma.

THE INTERRELATIONSHIP DIGRAPH

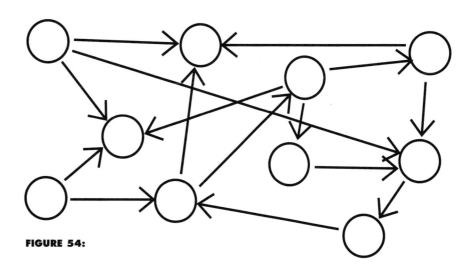

FIGURE 54:

E veryone, at one time or another, has been faced with a list of items that should be accomplished, but given only 1/4 the amount of time necessary to complete all of them. Faced with such a dilemma, one has two choices: partially address each item, or fully complete a portion of the items. In most cases, the most effective approach is the latter, fully complete some of the items. Selecting that approach, one is left with another fundamental issue; which items should be selected for attention?

A LAW OFFICE IMPROVEMENT PLAN

Four attorneys share an office facility. In October of each year, the four meet to establish a simple line-item budget for the coming calendar year. Each, in turn, agrees to provide a fourth of the fiscal revenues to support the budget. The most junior member of the group, Marion, was frustrated by her first such meeting the preceding year. The more senior attorneys were more aggressive in promoting their priorities, and she was left holding 1/4 the bill for an operation which she felt didn't benefit any of the group members. She wanted very much to do away with the power-play decision procedure of last year, and find a format of decision making that would objectively identify the primary, driving budget issues for the law office.

The interrelationship digraph (ID) is a management and planning tool which could help resolve the problem issues in both scenarios. The ID can be an effective tool:

- Anytime the **DRIVING** issues must be identified from a group of important issues,

- When limited resources require a **CAREFULLY FOCUSED EFFORT** to remedy the most portentous problems,

- When there is need to **IDENTIFY THE ROOT CAUSE(S)**,

- When there is an **INSUFFICIENT AMOUNT OF OBJECTIVE DATA** upon which to base a statistical decision.

The ID, when properly utilized, can provide a clear illustration of "what causes what." This is valuable when making a decision about which items to complete on a "to do" list. If you are able to identify a few tasks which, if completed, favorably affect the greatest number of other tasks, you can apply your efforts most effectively.

Having received training in the management and planning tools during an internship with a district attorney's office, Marion persuaded her three partners to analyze their office budget using the tools. While Marion had promoted the inclusion of all employees, she was advised that only the four attorneys would be involved.

She facilitated the group through an affinity diagram relating to the attorneys' needs from the office arrangement. After preparing a vast number of sticky notes, the group facilitated an affinity grouping of the notes and identified the following list of headers for the groupings of notes (in no specific priority order):

1. **EFFECTIVE COMMUNICATION SYSTEM.** This grouping included notes relating to clarity of phone messages, good secretarial skills in dealing with clients, functional telephone system, effective intra-office memo system, etc. Marion had fought hard last year for additional money for secretarial training and support, but was out-voted by those who preferred to spend that money on new carpeting and draperies.

2. **PROFESSIONAL IMAGE.** While Marion agreed that appearance is an important component of a client's perception of his/her legal counsel, she felt there was too much consideration given to the issue. Others in the group, obviously, had disagreed. In addition, there was talk of new panelling and art work from the upcoming year's budget.

3. **UP-TO-DATE LAW LIBRARY.** The conference room/law library of the office was in constant need of attention. Legal updates, changes in laws, and multiple legal publications required nearly constant attention, if the library was to be kept functional, orderly, and neat. Unfortunately, it regularly was in disarray due to the difficulty the secretaries had in completing other tasks.

4. **QUALITY DOCUMENT SUPPORT.** This header represented notes relating to proper spelling on correspondence and court documents, timely preparation and distribution of letters, easy-to-access filing system, timely filing of all documents into client files, etc.

5. **SCHEDULING.** Each of the attorneys had addressed this issue on at least one sticky note. Appropriate scheduling of office visits, vacation weeks, court appearances, and other obligations had caused distress among the attorneys, and between attorneys and secretaries.

6. **SOCIAL INTERACTION.** Everyone addressed this topic during the affinity note production. The benefit of being around other people was clearly important to all the attorneys.

7. **GROUP FRINGE BENEFITS.** Group health and life insurance, tax benefits of partnership, group membership discounts, etc. were included under this header.

Marion took the seven header notes and placed them around the surface of a large piece of chart paper. The notes displayed only an abbreviated version of each header issue, but the group reviewed the complete header statements to assure that all agreed on the issue definitions.

FIGURE 55:

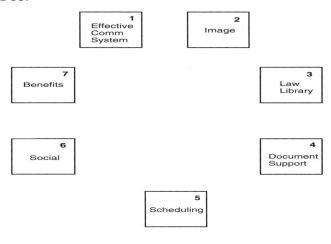

Beginning with question #1, she asked the group, "Does #1 tend to cause or influence #2?" Then, "Does #1 cause or influence #3?" She continued until the group had reached a consensus about whether question #1 caused or influenced each of the other header topics. When the group consensus was that #1 did cause or influence another header, an arrow was drawn from #1 to the affected header. If no cause or influence was associated, no arrow was drawn.

Marion then did the same in relation to question #2. If there was agreement that two headers were mutually influencing one another, the group would make a commitment based on which tended to cause the *most* influence. When a consensus was reached, the arrow was drawn *from* the one that influenced the most, and to the lesser influencing header. The attorneys' completed diagram looked like this:

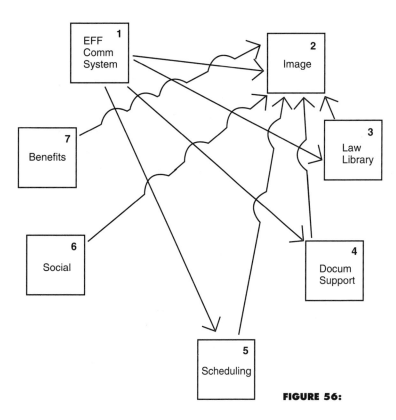

FIGURE 56:

Marion counted all of the incoming and outgoing arrows for each header card and documented the count on each header card. The arrow count tally was:

	INCOMING	OUTGOING
1. Effective Communication System	0	4
2. Professional Image	6	0
3. Up-to-Date Law Library	1	1
4. Quality Document Support	1	1
5. Scheduling	1	1
6. Social Interaction	0	1
7. Group Fringe Benefits	0	1

In analyzing the ID, look initially for headers with the largest number of **OUTGOING** arrows. As a general rule, these header topics are the "drivers" in your processes. The diagram documents the fact that your group feels that the driver issue is the one(s) which, if addressed, will have the greatest impact on the greatest number of other issues. The header issues with the greatest number of **INCOMING** arrows may also indicate an issue that needs attention, though it is less likely to be a real "effecter" issue.

Clearly, issue #1 is the one that seems to affect the greatest number of other issues. Professional image is obviously affected by all of the other issues, and would best be addressed, they all agreed, by enhancing as many of the other header issues as possible. The new panelling and art work, they concurred unanimously, could be put off in favor of other priorities. The group discussed various means of accomplishing the greatest number of header issues with the smallest possible monetary output.

The group discussion resulted in a realization that several important issues could potentially be addressed by providing better training and education opportunities for the secretaries. The communication system, quality of document support, scheduling, and professional image would probably all be positively influenced. An orderly law library would also enhance professional appearance during conferences with client groups.

In relation to issue 2 (professional image), the large number of incoming arrows indicates that issue is primarily an "outcome" of the other issues. An outcome issue may become a metric to determine if the other issues are being successfully addressed. In this case, a measurable improvement in "professional image" would likely be the result of successfully addressing the "drivers."

By all appearances, Marion had logically and persuasively supported her assertion that more money should be made available for staff training. While the group mutually agreed upon a solution (increase the training portion of the budget), there are other MP Tools that could be used, should the group have disagreed or felt unsure about what steps to take to resolve the priority issue(s).

If you feel uncomfortable with all the lines and arrows of the graphic ID (Figure 56), the Interrelationship Digraph can also be accomplished with a matrix format. The matrix is constructed by marking the header numbers along both the side and across the top of the grid:

		1	2	3	4	5	6	7	Total IN	Total OUT
EFFECTIVE COMMUNICATION SYSTEM	1	X	↑	↑	↑	↑			0	4
PROFESSIONAL IMAGE	2	←	X	←	←	←	←	←	6	0
UP-TO-DATE LAW LIBRARY	3	←	↑	X					1	1
QUALITY DOCUMENT SUPPORT	4	←	↑		X				1	1
SCHEDULING	5	←	↑			X			1	1
SOCIAL INTERACTION	6		↑				X		0	1
GROUP FRINGE BENEFITS	7		↑					X	0	1

FIGURE 57:

Once the matrix is constructed, move across horizontally, asking if 1 causes or influences 2, then does 1 cause or influence 3, and so on. If you determine that 1 does, in fact, cause or influence 3, you draw an arrow pointing up, in the box across from 1 and below 3. If you feel that 3 causes or influences 1, draw the arrow so it points to the left. All arrows will point up, or to the left. The diagram above is a matrix version of the attorneys' office scenario.

Be open minded when analyzing the outcome of an ID. Don't discard your ID simply because it doesn't reflect your anticipated or preferred outcome. Have faith in the process and be willing to make changes based on a more objective basis than intuition. Intuition certainly has its place in managing, but not necessarily in the face of clear data.

While Marion chose to use the header cards from an affinity diagram as the origin of the attorneys' issues, ID issues may come from:

- Group brainstorming and consensus
- Organizational objectives
- Customer complaints
- Other processes.

THE TREE DIAGRAM

FIGURE 58:

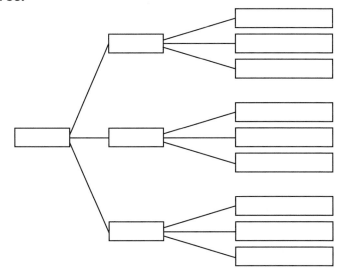

The tree diagram probably looks familiar. The same general format is used to illustrate organizational structures, single elimination competitions, and various other expanding or, in reverse order, diminishing numbers of sub-groups. The application of the tree diagram as a management and planning tool is consistent with the same general application.

If your organization has ever introduced a new product or service, or has ever implemented a new production process, you likely experienced the realization that it's difficult to predict all of the potential obstacles to that implementation. The tree diagram is a tool that allows an individual or group to formally map out a process, and to determine exactly what will need to be accomplished at each level of an organization for that process to be successfully implemented.

Similarly, a tree diagram can be used to illustrate the procedural and individual adjustments needed to successfully activate a new goal or policy within an organization.

In both circumstances (production processes and policy modification), the implementation traditionally begins once an apparently adequate policy or process is identified and prepared. Too often, unforeseen obstacles arise. Sometimes the accommodations for unplanned problems take far more personnel time and money than the original implementation planning. Such a situation may be as preventable as it is wasteful.

INVESTIGATING A CAMPUS UTILITIES CHANGEOVER

The tree diagram is used to expand a proposed change from a general idea to a specific series of actions. If conscientiously applied, a tree diagram process will identify specifically what each division or member of an organization will have to do to effectively facilitate a change in policy or process.

A comptroller for a university returned from a seminar relating to managing energy costs for educational institutions. He had taken heating cost data for the university from the preceding biennium, and had taken advantage of an opportunity to have an energy consultant review the data. He entered the university president's office and excitedly displayed the calculations which indicated a significant potential savings for the institution, should they convert from their current oil-fired furnaces to natural gas. The figures were produced in response to the comptroller's questions relating to cost of heat, per therm, for both energy sources. The potential savings appeared significant.

The president was impressed with the data. As a budding Total Quality Management executive, however, she knew that any such change must be studied by a carefully selected team. She notified the TQM coordinator about the issue, and the coordinator selected team members from the comptroller's office, the physical plant, the maintenance office, the physical science department, and the physics department. The coordinator, himself, would also function as a facilitator.

The following week, the team met to discuss the issue of changing heating energy sources for the university. The comptroller began the presentation with a summary of the projected savings involved, should the institution change over to natural gas.

After he sat down, the TQM coordinator stood and informed the team that their purpose was to analyze the institutional impact of such a change.

The physical plant supervisor informed the group that a conversion from oil to gas would probably require more than simply converting the fuel lines from an oil tank to a gas line. In addition, there was the expense of digging up and disposing of the huge, old underground oil tanks. Assuming there would be some amount of leakage during the process, an environmental cleanup team might be needed. If the old tanks had already leaked oil into soil, a more extensive cleanup would be required.

"If leakage has taken place," the physical science instructor suggested, "we should aggressively move toward the resolution of that, regardless of our decision to convert energy sources. We have a commitment to society."

"I think we all agree about that point, but we're here to look at the overall impact of the suggested conversion from one energy source to another," the coordinator indicated.

"Let's list the areas," he continued, drawing a small rectangle on the left side of a large chalk board on the wall of the meeting room, "of the impact of the suggested change from oil to gas."

"Well, it's clear that we have to consider the expense of cleaning up any oil-related contamination," the physical plant supervisor repeated.

The coordinator wrote "conversion, oil to gas" in the small box he had drawn on the board. He drew a short line from the right side of that box, and drew another box at the end of the line. In the second box he wrote "clean up oil."

"And what about the expense of installing gas lines into the physical plant?" Asked the physics department representative.

Directly above the "cleanup oil" box, the TQM coordinator drew another box and wrote "install gas lines" in it.

"It's not just the expense of installation," another team member added, "What about the disruption of foot and car traffic around the physical plant during the construction process?"

"We haven't even talked about maintaining constant heat during the changeover," the science representative stated. "That could be crucial to some of the areas where controlled environments are critical."

The team continued to brainstorm about the impact of the changeover. The comptroller was somewhat surprised at the significant impact that the implementation of the energy conversion would have on the operation of the institution.

"Look, it seemed like a good idea at first, but I didn't realize how extensive the impact would be. Maybe we should just wait until there's a more critical need before we jump into this," the comptroller recommended.

"Believe me," the TQM coordinator voiced, "every change has multiple areas of impact. The fact that this issue is more complex than initially believed doesn't mean it should be abandoned. Besides, trying to conduct this study during a period of urgent need would greatly reduce our flexibility of implementation. Let's continue until we've looked at the overall impact of the recommended change."

The team produced a small group of general areas of impact, should the energy source conversion take place. The diagram now looked like this:

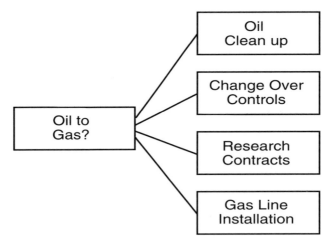

FIGURE 59:

"The next step in our investigation," the coordinator advised the team, "is look at each of these four areas and ask, 'what must be done to accomplish this?' Why don't we start at the top of the chart? What must be done to accomplish the oil system clean-up?"

The team continued to discuss the various activities which would have to be completed to accomplish the cleanup of the old oil storage tanks and feed lines. By the time the team was finished with their initial meeting, they had completed the oil cleanup limb of their tree diagram as follows:

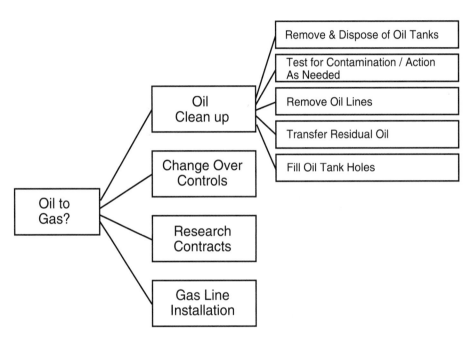

FIGURE 60:

During subsequent meetings, the team completed the tree diagram. They reviewed the completed diagram by starting at the far right (specific activities) branches for each main branch and asking, "If all of these are attained, will the next, larger branch be accomplished?" If the team determines that they haven't left out any important actions, and the answer is a confident "yes" for each set of branches, the team can feel assured that the initial issue will be successfully illustrated or implemented by following the steps in the diagram.

The team selected the comptroller and the physical plant supervisor to present the team's product to the president. The initial impact and expense of the changeover was more extensive than initially anticipated. The period of recovering the change-over cost with reduced utility bills would be longer than first projected. The president, however, now had a realistic perception of the issue, and would be far less likely to be surprised by unanticipated expenses and delays should the project be approved.

The tree diagram is equally effective at illustrating the steps necessary to accomplish a new or modified manufacturing process. A well-planned production process change can be implemented with amazing efficiency when every member of the production group is provided with detailed, personal activity requirements. Trial-and-error modifications can be greatly reduced or eliminated.

When initially brainstorming the basic and subsequent specific actions necessary to complete a goal (the "trunk" of the tree diagram), consider writing the recommended actions on note cards (Post-It™ Notes work very well). This allows the group to move the action notes around without having to erase or start over. Often, actions that initially seem to constitute their own "limb" will be later identified as a sub-set of limbs for another major set of actions. With the actions on note cards or Post-Its™, the realigning of tree limbs is much quicker and easier.

The stress and inefficiency associated with change can be diminished by reducing the amount of mystery associated with it.

Had you begun resolving a problem using the affinity, followed by the interrelationship digraph, and identified two or three primary issues upon which you needed to focus your attention, you could now use a tree diagram to continue your planning. The tree would provide you a method with which you can turn the general topics into detailed action plans.

Whether you apply the tree as an evaluation tool (like the university illustration) or an implementation tool for a production process, you'll benefit from the logical manner by which it allows you to plan thoroughly and effectively.

PRIORITIZATION MATRIX

The traditional symbol for the prioritization matrix looks like this:

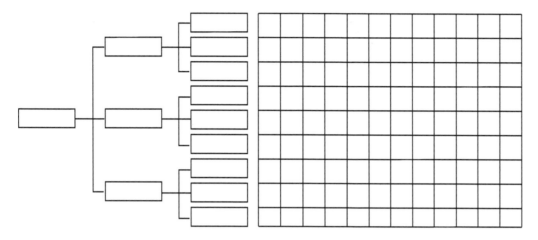

FIGURE 61:

As the name of this management and planning tool implies, it is used to select the best of a number of options by giving you a means of prioritizing those options. If you want to buy a new car, for example, you have a pretty good idea what optional equipment items you want, which color you prefer, how much room you need, etc. All of those elements are the **CRITERIA** you apply to the various **OPTIONS** (different cars). When a group needs to make a decision about which item to purchase, or what qualities to consider in hiring new employees, etc.; the process of determining criteria becomes somewhat more difficult. Each person has a different perspective about which criteria are the most important.

THE PRIORITIZATION MATRIX ALLOWS A GROUP TO:

1. **IDENTIFY WHICH CRITERIA** should be considered in selecting an option,

2. **PRIORITIZE THOSE CRITERIA** by determining a relative numerical score for each criteria (the most important criterion will have the highest criterion score),

3. **RANK AND SCORE THE RELATIVE IMPORTANCE OF EACH OPTION** (the most preferred option will display the highest option-ranking score),

4. **COMBINE THE CRITERIA SCORE AND THE OPTION SCORE** to determine which of the various options you will pursue, buy, hire, etc.

You probably recognize the left side of this symbol as a tree diagram. The tree diagram allows a general goal to be broken down to the specific acts that must be accomplished to meet that goal. Once a tree diagram is completed, the outer limbs identify the specific acts you or your organization must perform. It doesn't, however, identify which are the most important, or which should be done first. The prioritization matrix can be applied to identify which items are the most critical, or which option(s) you should pursue.

There are several methods of constructing a prioritization matrix. You may read about:

- The full analytical method
- The consensus method
- The combined interrelationship digraph/matrix method.

As intimidating as the method names sound, there are only a few, relatively simple steps involved in each. For the purpose of this chapter, let's look at the consensus method in some detail.

The word consensus means "general agreement." Fortunately, it isn't necessary for all group members to reach agreement to utilize this method. Instead, each member's personal priority is documented and a single, overall group score will emerge.

A hair salon needed to purchase new barber/styling chairs. Five hair stylists, including the manager, met to decide which model of chair to purchase. They used a tree diagram to develop the specific criteria desired in the ideal chair. The tree looked like this:

CHOOSING THE BEST SALON CHAIR (CONSENSUS METHOD)

FIGURE 62:

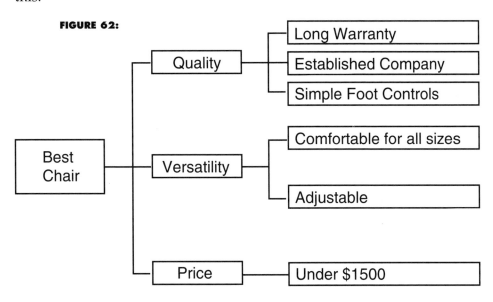

The tree diagram has allowed the group of stylists to express the specific criteria they want to consider when deciding which chair to purchase. In that the manager, Dave, is truly a customer-oriented businessman, he recognizes that the stylists are his most immediate customers. The stylists, in turn, recognize that the paying customer is the most important consideration in their decision process. Because of this, the criterion of price may be rated lower than it might be in a less customer-oriented business.

With a mutually acceptable set of criteria, the group is ready to prioritize them. Dave explains that he wants each stylist to look at the list of criteria and decide which is most important, which is second, and so on. To simplify the process, he tells the stylists to assume they each have one dollar (one hundred pennies) in front of them. The group members are told to determine how many of the pennies each would place on each criterion. The most important criterion would be given the most pennies. If a member believes a single criterion is much more important than the others, (s)he may give half or more of the pennies to that criterion. Once the stylists had distributed their imaginary pile of pennies, Dave began to compile the data, and record each stylist's distribution.

The total score for each criterion is calculated by adding each stylist's penny total for each criterion. That total will be added to the summary matrix which will soon be constructed.

FIGURE 63:

	Dave	Lisa	Julie	Shannon	Rhonda	Total
Long Warranty	.30	.40	.20	.20	.30	1.40
Established Co.	.30	.20	.20	.10	.10	0.90
Simple controls	.10	.05	.40	.10	.20	0.85
Comfort for all	.20	.20	.10	.30	.20	1.00
Adjustable	.05	.05	.05	.10	.10	0.35
Price	.05	.10	.05	.20	.10	0.50

Next, Dave presented manufacturers' pamphlets for each of the five chair models currently available. All five of the stylists were sufficiently familiar with styling-chair technology to make an informed evaluation of the chairs' relative merits. Dave listed the chairs as options A, B, C, D, and E. He requested each team member to assign a "1" to the chair option (s)he thought was the **LEAST** preferred in relation to criterion 1 (Warranty), a "2" by the one that was second least preferred, etc. In this way, the chair with the most preferred warranty would have a score of "5" (since there are five options).

The team members rated the chair options as follows, based on each chairs' compliance with team members' perception of "long warranty." The warranty criteria rating for the chair options looked like this:

FIGURE 64:

Warranty	Dave	Lisa	Julie	Shannon	Rhonda	Total	Rank
Chair A	2	1	3	2	2	10	4th
Chair B	5	5	4	5	4	23	1st
Chair C	1	2	2	1	1	7	5th
Chair D	4	3	1	3	3	14	3rd
Chair E	3	4	5	4	5	21	2nd

Based on warranty, the team's consensus rating places chair B as the chair that most closely meets their needs for long warranty (it has the highest total score, 23). Chair C, obviously rates last among the chairs when considering warranty only (lowest total score, 7). These scores are retained for use in a summary matrix.

The team will conduct another ranking of the chair options based on the criterion of "established company." Additional consensus rankings will be completed for the chair options based on each of the remaining criteria (simple controls, comfort for all, adjustable, and price). Since there are **SIX** criteria, the team will prepare a total of **SIX** consensus-ranking charts. If the team had identified eight criteria for the chair selection process, they would need to prepare eight ranking charts.

The summary matrix for the salon chair prioritization process displays the chair options down the left side, and the criteria across the top. Dave produced the original criteria ranking scored (from Figure 63) and transfers the criteria scores to the summary matrix. The appropriate consensus ranking numbers are added below each of the criterion.

In each box of the matrix, Dave and his co-workers simply multiply the listed criterion ranking score times the consensus ranking number. As you see below, the box formed at the intersection of "Warranty" and Chair option "A" contains the warranty criterion ranking score of 1.4, and the consensus ranking number of 2, making the overall score for that box 2.80.

The data from all the matrices are transferred to the summary matrix, which produces the following chart:

FIGURE 65:

Chair Option / Criteria	Warranty 1.4	Estab'd Co. .90	Simple Controls .85	Comfort 1.0	Adjustable .35	Price .50	TOTAL
A	2 x 1.4 = 2.80	3 x .90 = 2.70	2 x .85 = 1.70	4 x 1.0 = 4.00	2 x .35 = .70	3 x .50 = 1.50	13.40
B	5 x 1.4 = 7.00	4 x .90 = 3.60	4 x .85 = 3.40	5 x 1.0 = 5.00	4 x .35 = 1.40	5 x .50 = 2.50	22.90 1st choice
C	1 x 1.4 = 2.80	2 x .90 = 1.80	3x .85 = 2.55	3 x 1.0 = 3.00	3 x .35 = 1.05	1 x .50 = .50	11.70
D	3 x 1.4 = 4.20	1 x .90 = .90	1 x .85 = .85	1 x 1.0 = 1.00	1 x .35 = .35	2 x .50 = 1.00	8.30
E	4 x 1.4 = 5.60	5 x .90 = 4.50	5 x .85 = 4.25	2 x 1.0 = 2.00	5 x .35 = 1.75	4 x .50 = 2.00	20.10 2nd choice

Based on the groups use of the consensus prioritization matrix, the highest rated chair is chair option B, which has the highest score (22.90). If, for some reason, that chair isn't available, chair option E is a close second (score of 20.10) and would be the next best choice.

FIGURE 66:

Criteria / Options	1	2	3	4
A				
B				
C				
D				

The prioritization matrix displays the options down the left side, and the criteria across the top. Each square in the matrix now contains the criteria priority score and the option ranking score. The two are multiplied together to create the total score for each option. Generally, the option with the highest score is the appropriate choice. The matrix has allowed the team of stylists to not only consider what qualities they want in a styling chair, but how to effectively utilize the variation in criteria importance.

The prioritization matrix can be used equally well to make decisions about raw materials choices, training and educational opportunities, program decisions, and just about any process that requires a group to identify a prioritized list of issues/items for which there are multiple criteria for selection.

FULL ANALYTICAL DIGRAPH MATRIX

The full analytical method of the prioritization matrix also involves multiple matrices. A separate matrix is employed to produce the criteria importance scores by applying a matrix to compare each criterion to all other criteria (see Figure 67). The scores produced reflect the actual relative value of each criterion (rather than the simple ranking of the consensus method). Those scores are set aside and will be used in a final summary matrix.

FIGURE 67:

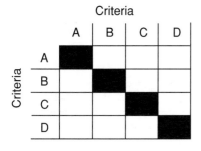

Next, a matrix is constructed listing all the options down the left side *and* across the top of the matrix. Thinking in terms of the first criterion, you compare each option to all the other options, asking, "How does option A compare to option B in terms of the first criterion? And option A to option C?" And so on until you have compared every option. Once all the options have been compared to every other option on the basis of their relative worth according to criterion 1, additional matrices are constructed, one for each criterion. When using the full analytical method, you will produce as many of these option-to-criteria matrices as the number of criteria you want to consider. By mathematically combining the various individual matrix scores, a summary matrix is produced.

INTERRELATIONSHIP DIGRAPH MATRIX

The interrelationship digraph/matrix method is another single matrix format that employs general group consensus regarding which options have the greatest level of influence. You may recall that the interrelationship digraph (ID) is used to determine which issues are "driving" or "causing" issues, and which are "results." The ID/matrix simply utilizes a graphic ID (Figure

57) to compare each option with all other options based on which causes or influences the other. A relative strength of influence is also assigned. The interpretation of the ID/matrix is somewhat more subjective than the easily identifiable numerical scores produced by the consensus and full analytical methods.

While these ridiculously abbreviated descriptions have probably left you thinking you never want to try the full analytical method, it is the most effective method to apply in many circumstances, and much simpler when addressed one step at a time with complete instructions. A more detailed description of each of the prioritization matrix methods is available in the *Memory Jogger Plus+®*, available through GOAL/QPC.

No matter which method you choose to apply, the prioritization matrix is a tool that can provide you with a reliable and well thought-out prioritization of numerous options.

THE MATRICES

■ ■ ■ ■ ■ ■

I n the preceding chapter, you were introduced to a tool called the prioritization matrix (PM). That tool was presented as a means of comparing a group of possible options to a list of criteria. The PM is simply a specific use, L-shaped matrix. There are a variety of other applications of the L-shaped matrix as well. This section of the MP Tools will describe some of those other L-shaped matrix applications, and introduce you to additional matrix formats as well.

THE MATRICES ARE OFTEN USED TO:

- **ASSIGN TASKS** to individuals involved in a group effort,

- **SCORE ITEMS FOR COMPARISON** (like the prioritization matrix),

- **ORGANIZE LARGE NUMBERS OF DATA GROUPS** for comparison,

- **IDENTIFY RELATIONSHIP PATTERNS** in groups of issues,

- And a wide variety of similar applications.

A common application of the L-shaped matrix involves the assignment of a series of tasks to a group of people. For the purpose of this illustration, let's assume that you are a member of a civic organization making preparations for a large convention to be held in your home town. A committee of six people, including you, meet to begin the planning process.

CONVENTION COMMITTEE ASSIGNMENTS

The convention will bring a large number of people into town, and a number of issues must be investigated to make sure all the appropriate accommodations are available and ready. With the group together, you initiate a brainstorming discussion to identify the issues that need to be researched before the plans can proceed further.

The following list of issues are identified by you and the other group members:

1. Number and location of available hotel/motel rooms
2. Number and location of meeting rooms
3. Availability of transportation from airport to town
4. Conference keynote speaker
5. Registration location and staffing
6. Schedule of commercial displays
7. Determine registration fee
8. Set up event fiscal control
9. Solicit donation for door prizes and drawings

While the list is fairly general at this point, you simply want to begin the process of gathering information. Much more detailed lists of tasks will be constructed as the convention nears.

With a list of the initial tasks, and a group of six people to whom you can assign the tasks, you recommend that the group apply an L-shaped matrix to identify at least one person to complete each task. A benefit of this application of a matrix is the ease with which it allows the group to assign primary responsibility for a task, as well as secondary responsibility. You can also use the matrix to document who will be kept informed about the progress in each of the nine task areas.

There are three traditional symbols used to identify these varying levels of responsibility: primary, secondary, and keep informed (Figure 68).

These same symbols are used to represent other qualities with up to three levels of variation (e.g., very important, somewhat important, not important; or significant impact/affect, some impact or affect, and no impact/affect, etc.).

The committee members are Aaron, Dennis, Casey, Miriam, Liese, and you, Jordan. You construct an L-shaped matrix with your group members' names across the top (x axis), and the tasks along the left side (y axis) as in Figure 69.

FIGURE 68:

Primary
Responsibility

Secondary
Responsibility

Keep
Informed

CONVENTION COMMITTEE ASSIGNMENT MATRIX

PERSON / TASK	Dennis	Casey	Aaron	Liese	Miriam	Jordan
# / location of rooms						
" " meeting rooms						
airport transportation						
keynote speaker						
regist. place / staff						
commercial displays						
registration costs						
fiscal control						
prizes / drawings						

FIGURE 69:

The group discusses which, if any, of the issues each individual wants to investigate, or whether any group member has special knowledge in any of the areas. You, for example, are vice-president of a local bank, so you offer to be primarily responsible for researching the fiscal control needed for the convention funds. You also have a number of contacts with local business people and offer to accept secondary responsibility for the task of soliciting prizes for drawings. Since you will be contacting businesses, including motels/hotels, for prize donations, you also agree to accept a secondary role in the research of room and meeting facility topics.

Each of the group members accepts other responsibilities, and Liese indicates a willingness to coordinate the efforts to guarantee that all the tasks will be investigated before your next meeting. Liese will be identified as the one to be kept advised for all the tasks.

The completed task assignment matrix looks like Figure 70.

PERSON / TASK	Dennis	Casey	Aaron	Liese	Miriam	Jordan
# / location of rooms				△	●	○
" " meeting rooms				△	●	○
airport transportation	●		○	○		
keynote speaker	●			○		
regist. place / staff			○	△	●	
commercial displays		●		△		
registration costs		●		△	○	
fiscal control		○		△		●
prizes / drawings	○		●	△		○

FIGURE 70:

Because of her ability to coordinate and supervise, Liese will be kept advised of all the other group members' activities. She accepts two secondary roles, but will basically be responsible for seeing that the tasks are completed in a timely manner, and that all persons involved in a task know the progress made by every other member. This "coordinator" role is not mandatory, and may not be needed for many applications of the task assignment matrix.

A copy of this task assignment matrix will be provided to each member of the team, so every individual involved knows who to contact about each task.

The L-shaped matrix can be used anytime you have one set of variables which you wish to compare to one other set of variables.

Another matrix format is the "T-shaped" matrix, which allows the user to compare one list of variables against two other sets of variables. A T-shaped matrix is an excellent format, for example, to compare two options against a specific set of criteria.

A business, in the process of selecting a communication company from which to purchase a telephone system, might appropriately choose to utilize a T-shaped matrix to make the selection process more efficient.

SELECTING A BUSINESS PHONE SYSTEM

The business manager believes the business needs a system that will provide basic business service: multiple incoming lines, a central answering unit, an internal communication capacity, forwarding of calls, call holding, etc. Aware of rapid advancements in the communication industry, the business also wants some guarantee of upgradability in their communication system.

The business manager calls a staff meeting and asks for input regarding preferred characteristics in a communication system. His perceptions of his employees' needs were fairly accurate, but a few additional needs surface in the meeting. By the time the staff meeting breaks up, the following list of communication needs has been compiled:

1. Call forward
2. Call transfer
3. Central call reception
4. Multiple line phones
5. Conference call capacity
6. Multiple pre-programmed numbers
7. Hands free capacity
8. Internal "Com" line

Two communication companies have provided information about systems which they believe will meet the needs of the business. The information relating to the characteristics of each system have been provided to the business owner. The owner will, individually or with a group of staff, construct a matrix with the available information.

The desired characteristics that the employees generated will be written vertically in the middle of a piece of paper. The system characteristics of one phone system are written horizontally to the left of the desired characteristics list, and the system characteristics of the second system is placed on the right. The T-shaped matrix formed looks like Figure 71.

Each company offers several optional phone systems. Each offers an increasing variety of services as the system options become more sophisticated and expensive. The objective of the employees is to determine which of the two communication companies' phone system options will meet their needs for the least expense.

CUSTOM SYSTEM	OPTION 3	OPTION 2	OPTION 1	BASIC SYSTEM	Our Phone Needs	BASIC SYSTEM	OPTION 1	OPTION 2	OPTION 3	CUSTOM SYSTEM
					Forwarding					
					Transfering					
					Central Reception					
					Multiple Lines					
					Conference					
					Programmable Calls					
					No Hands					
					Com Line					

Communication Company A — Communication Company B

FIGURE 71:

The manager chooses to call another staff meeting to fill out the matrix. Each employee reviews the communication companies' various systems. As a group, the employees identify which of their needs are filled by each company's system options. The process is time-consuming, but not difficult.

The employees determine that each communication company has a basic system and three package options, as well as an option to construct a customized system for the business. The cost of each system increases, obviously, as the services improve. Both communication company's base systems and standard options are similarly priced, so the determining factor will be which company's system meets all or most of the business' needs at the lowest option number (lowest price).

By reviewing the base systems first, the employees determine that company B's base system meets one of their needs, and somewhat meets a second, while company A's base system only somewhat meets one need. In a hurry, an individual or group might assume that company B will provide the best system for the lowest price. The group continues, however, to review each optional system for both companies.

By the time the group has reviewed each system option, and plotted the information on their T-shaped matrix, the product matrix looks like Figure 72.

| Communication Company A | | | | | Our Phone Needs | Communication Company B | | | | |
CUSTOM SYSTEM	OPTION 3	OPTION 2	OPTION 1	BASIC SYSTEM		BASIC SYSTEM	OPTION 1	OPTION 2	OPTION 3	CUSTOM SYSTEM
●	●	●	●	△	Forwarding	△	△	○	●	●
●	●	●	●	△	Transfering	△	○	○	○	●
●	●	●	●	○	Central Reception	●	●	●	●	●
●	●	●	○	△	Multiple Lines	△	○	○	●	●
●	●	●	○	△	Conference	△	△	○	●	●
●	●	●	●	△	Programmable Calls	△	○	●	●	●
●	●	●	●	△	No Hands	○	●	●	●	●
●	●	●	○	△	Com Line	△	○	●	●	●

● Meets / Exceeds   ○ Somewhat Meets   △ Does Not Meet

FIGURE 72:

Perhaps to the surprise of some individuals, company A's option 2 system meets or exceeds all of the business' phone system needs. While company B offers a variety of great services with each option, they aren't able to meet all of the business' needs without the construction of an expensive, custom phone system.

The T-shaped matrix is a clear and logical format by which two multi-faceted options can be effectively compared to a single list of needs.

THERE ARE A VARIETY OF OTHER MATRIX FORMATS INCLUDING:

A. THE Y-SHAPED MATRIX - Also allows for the comparison of three sets of data. Unlike the T-shaped matrix which allows for the comparison of two sets of options to a single set of criteria, the Y-shaped matrix allows the user to compare each of three sets of data to the other two sets.

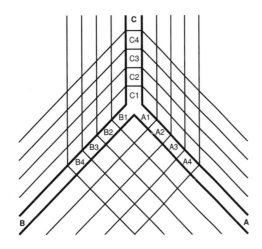

FIGURE 73:

B. THE C-SHAPED MATRIX - Similar to the Y-shaped matrix in layout, this matrix format allows the user to compare the interrelationship of three sets of data, and to three dimensionally plots where, among those three sets of data, the best combined option exists.

C. THE X-SHAPED MATRIX - An infrequently utilized tool, this format provides a framework by which four different data sets can be plotted, and each set can be compared to two of the other sets.

If you are involved in a business that you believe requires the application of these more sophisticated matrices, contact GOAL/QPC for information relating to advanced MP Tools resources or training.

THE PROCESS DECISION PROGRAM CHART (PDPC)

■ ■ ■ ■ ■ ■

While planning for problem-free actions is a basic concern for all TQM business activities, there are certain processes that require special planning and implementation efforts. The PDPC is a tool which allows you to identify likely problem spots in your planned process, and prepare alternative actions, in case those likely problems occur. **YOU MAY WANT TO UTILIZE THIS TOOL WHEN:**

- You're planning for **A NEW PROCESS**,

- The process for which you are planning is **COMPLEX**,

- The **RISK OR COST OF FAILURE** during implementation is **HIGH**,

- You have **LIMITED TIME OR RESOURCES** for implementation.

The PDPC is a graphic tool and requires only writing instruments and surface, in addition to a thorough understanding of the process to be implemented.

The form of the PDPC is essentially a tree diagram with an additional set of limbs attached to actions which have a reasonable likelihood of variation or failure. Once those potential problem actions are identified, alternative actions are prepared. If the alternate actions can be implemented as preventive measures, they can prevent problems from arising. If the process must be initiated before you have enough information to implement the alternate action(s), the alternate actions are held in ready, should the original action fail.

The most obvious value of this kind of planning is the time saved if and when a problem does arise. With a contingency plan at the ready, problems are much less likely to create wasteful, expensive "down time."

A TROUBLE-FREE HOME DELIVERY SYSTEM

A local restaurant decided to begin a home delivery service. A careful analysis of their customers' needs indicated that home delivery would provide a desirable service, and increase the number of people who would have an opportunity to experience the excellent food offered by the restaurant.

Because home delivery was an entirely new process for the restaurant, the owner decided to prepare a PDPC with the help of his employees. An initial tree diagram was prepared detailing the home delivery system: packaging materials and equipment, phone service, delivery vehicles, insurance, etc. The food ordering, preparation, and packaging were easily planned actions. The action of getting the food from the restaurant to the customer seemed to be the one area that held a number of potential pitfalls. No matter how good the food was at the time of packaging, a significant delay in delivery would result in decreased product quality.

An additional tree diagram was prepared, detailing the steps in the delivery process. That tree diagram looked like Figure 74.

FIGURE 74:

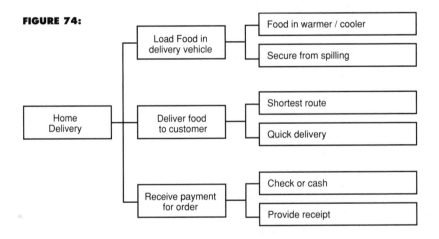

While examining the delivery process for potential problems, the owner suggests that each employee think about what might reasonably go wrong during each step in the tree diagram. While some people believe that presupposing problems is "negative thinking," it can become the most valuable part of the planning process.

An important aspect of this step is to restrict the "what if's" to those problems that are **REASONABLY** likely to occur. It can be counter-productive to ponder all the problems which could "possibly" occur.

One employee, who had previously worked as a home delivery person for a grocery store, recalled the problems involved with customers who were surprised at the amount of their bill. Those situations required a significant amount of time to remedy, as the delivery person sometimes needed to remove a few items and recalculate the customer's billing. The group determined that the surprised customer problem could be prevented by advising the customer of the amount of the bill at the time the order was placed. As a result of another employees suggestion, the order taker could also advise the customer of the acceptable manner of payment.

Because speedy delivery affected both customer satisfaction and food quality, the problem of delays from street closures, bridge construction, etc. could cause potentially avoidable problems. It would be simple, one employee suggested, to contact the city streets department each afternoon to get an update of road closures, which could be posted near the back delivery loading area.

The group continued to discuss a variety of likely problems associated with the home delivery process. By the time they finished, they had a series of actions to add to the PDPC. Since some of the actions are "prevention steps," they will be incorporated as standardized steps in the delivery format. Others are contingencies, for which alternate processes will be developed, in case the problem does arise. In those cases, everyone knows how to react, and can resolve the problem in a consistent, pre-planned manner.

The restaurant employees' final PDPC looked like Figure 75.

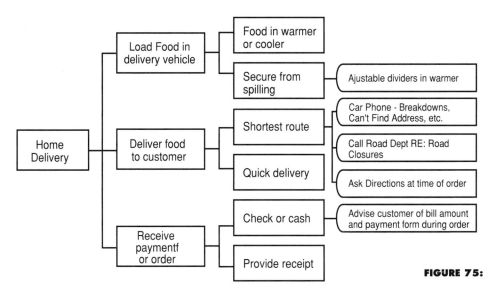

FIGURE 75:

The contingency steps are placed on the tree diagram in a form that allows them to be visually identified as contingency steps. The PDPC above uses a crescent shape to designate the step as an alternate action. Any form can be used, as long as it clearly identifies the alternative actions from the primary planned actions.

There is an outline format for constructing the PDPC as well. If, for some reason, you don't wish to use the diagram method, the outline format may be employed with equal efficiency. Most people will choose to use the diagram form because of it's simplicity and clarity. If, however, you would rather use the outline format, look in Michael Brassard's *Memory Jogger Plus+®*, available through GOAL/QPC.

Since most plans involve actions and processes with which we are familiar, the PDPC may not be necessary for every one. When new, unique, or high risk action plans are being prepared, however, the PDPC can be an invaluable part of the planning process.

THE ACTIVITY NETWORK

Any project that requires the completion of more than one activity can become delayed as one step in the project is postponed until a preceding step is completed. This kind of delay is always a waste of resources, and is frequently preventable through careful project planning.

SUCH DELAYS CAN BE PREVENTED BY:

- Carefully **IDENTIFYING ALL THE ACTIVITIES** required to complete a project,

- **IDENTIFYING THE AMOUNT OF TIME** required to complete each activity,

- **DETERMINING WHICH ACTIVITIES CAN OCCUR INDEPENDENTLY**, and which must be preceded by other activities,

- And by using the above data to **IDENTIFY THE EARLIEST AND LATEST** effective start and finish time for each activity.

The activity network provides a framework that utilizes each of the above elements to create a well planned network of activities which, when performed, constitute the most timely completion of the project.

Nearly all organizations have some form of written procedures and directives. Most, unfortunately, are a compilation of independent "orders" which are difficult or impossible to identify in terms of their movement toward the organization's mission. While the implementation of TQM into the organizational character tends to remedy that problem over time, there may immediately exist the need to provide some form of direction within every organization.

IMPLEMENTING A DIRECTIVE

Assuming you are the personnel director of an organization, and that you have a need to quickly implement a particular directive, you might benefit from the product of an activity network. In order to identify the most expeditious implementation schedule, you call a meeting of various representatives in your organization. Each member provides you a unique perspective, and represents a distinctive aspect of your organization's make-up.

Included are representatives from administration, the various employee unions, and middle managers. In a very small organization, this may mean you and your spouse, but for the purpose of illustration, let's assume each member is from a different department.

Once you have told the group about your recommended addition to the organization's directives manual, you receive responses relating to the group members' suggested process of review. While no one seems totally opposed to the directive, there are a series of "hoops" through which you will need to jump to create a true and sincere acceptance of the directive. Recognizing that every employee to be affected by the directive should be given an opportunity to provide input, you had intended to post draft copies and invite responses. Following your meeting, you have a much more extensive series of group reviews than you had anticipated.

In order to obtain a favorable tax benefit, the directive must be formally in place within a relatively short period of time, so you need to expedite the process to be completed within 30 days.

After the meeting, you are left with the following list of actions which should precede the issuance of the final directive:

1. Initial draft distribution to all managers,
2. Initial draft distribution to all union representatives,
3. Initial draft distribution to administration,
4. Receive all comments,
5. Re-draft directive as needed,
6. Distribute amended draft to managers,
7. Distribute amended draft to administration,
8. Distribute amended draft to union representatives,
9. Receive final recommendations,
10. Prepare final draft,
11. Research all directives for impact by new directive,
12. Distribute and initiate new directive.

While such a list of actions might seem to assure months of slow progress toward finalization of your directive, a workable time frame can be established.

To begin the activity network process, write each of the steps on the top half of a sticky back note. Also indicate the amount of time that will be required to complete that task. Once that's accomplished, prepare one note that says "**START**," and one that says "**COMPLETE**." Working on a flat surface (desk top, etc.) or an upright surface (wall, etc.), place the "**START**" note on the far left side of the work surface.

Place the first task that must be completed immediately to the right of "**START**." In this illustration, there are three actions which can be conducted at the same time (initial draft distributions.) Such "concurrent" actions (those which can take place at the same time) will be charted to illustrate the fact that they are taking place together. At this point, place all three "initial distribution" notes in a column.

FIGURE 76:

Continue to place each of the action notes to the right in the order in which they must be completed. A long range task, like "research all directives..." can be placed above or below the general line of actions.

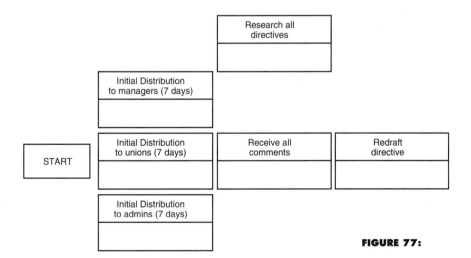

FIGURE 77:

Continue to place all the task notes on your work surface until they are all in place. Look carefully for tasks that could be completed while other tasks are under way, and place any of those tasks somewhere other than in the line between "**START**" and the end of your process, where you can now place the "**COMPLETE**" note.

Your completed set of notes (numbers correspond to list on Page 110) will look something like Figure 78.

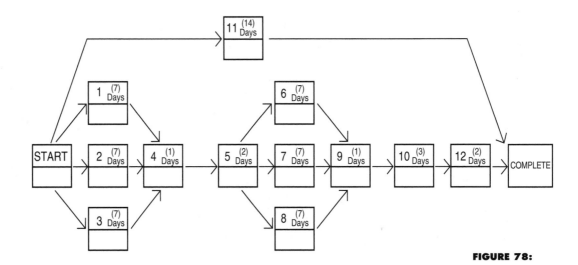

FIGURE 78:

By allowing the ongoing, long term action(s) to take place during other activities, the overall process will be significantly shorter than it would have been if you had chosen to complete them **BETWEEN** other action steps. Just like a construction company that tries to schedule the completion of a building in the shortest possible time, you will usually benefit by calculating and maintaining the shortest possible completion schedule for your projects.

At this point, you are relatively certain that you have prepared the shortest time line for completion of your directive process, but there is nothing to indicate the amount of time that will be required to complete all the tasks.

As you recall, we left the lower half of the task notes blank. At this point, divide that blank portion into four sections: (earliest start) (earliest finish) (latest start) (latest finish).

TASK & completion time	
(earliest start)	(earliest finish)
(latest start)	(latest finish)

FIGURE 79:

The four sections will be used to record the latest start and finish dates, and the earliest start and finish dates for each task.

Assuming you want to have the directive amended as necessary, and in-place within one month, you are ready to calculate the earliest and latest start and finish dates.

The final task note, "distribute and initiate new directive" must be completed no later than the 30th day of the process, in order to meet the one month deadline. The latest completion date section of that note can be filled in with "30." Since that action takes two days to complete, the latest start date for "distribute and initiate new directive" is the 28th day of the process. You can fill in the latest start date section with "28." Moving backward through the line of notes, you can calculate the latest start and finish dates for each of the tasks. Simply use the "latest start date" of the note to the right as the latest finish date for the adjacent note to the left.

For example, the latest start date for "distribute and initiate new directive" is day 28. Day 28, then, becomes the latest finish date for "prepare final draft," because the final draft must be prepared before the distribution can take place, but it can potentially be finalized on the same date that the next step begins.

Since the final draft preparation task takes three days, subtract 3 from 28 to get the latest start date for "prepare final draft." Day 25 is therefore the latest day that you can start that action, and still finish the project on time. Continue to work backwards through the notes until you reach the first task note(s), "initial distribution."

If you reach day "0" before you get back to the first task note, you don't have time to complete the project, even if you start immediately. While such a disclosure may sound like a terrible revelation, it's a lot better to find it out now than to find your nearly completed project delayed, illustrating your inadequate initial planning.

In the case of our illustration, we have some time built in to provide a buffer (7 days). The total project buffer period is the latest start time for task number 1. In essence, you could wait up to 7 days to begin the project, assuming your estimates for task duration are correct, and still complete the project on the 30th day.

Since few of us are interested in waiting until the very last second to begin a project, you can also calculate the earliest start and finish times for each task. Obviously, the earliest start time for any action is right now! Therefore, the earliest start time for tasks 1, 2, and 3 in our illustration is today, or day "0." Place a "0" in the earliest start time section of those three task notes. The earliest finish time, then, for each of those tasks is the 7th day, since they are projected to take 7 days to complete. The 7th day, therefore, becomes the earliest day that you could start the next consecutive task (receive all comments). Continue to calculate the earliest start and finish times for each task.

The final activity network diagram for your directive process is illustrated below.

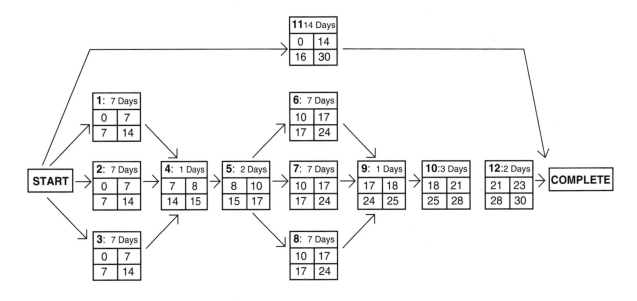

FIGURE 80:

At any point during the 30 day implementation schedule, you can easily determine whether you are ahead of schedule, or falling behind and unlikely to complete the project on time. Simply determine which day of the project you have reached. If you are at day 10, and the latest start time for the project you're working on is 10 or larger, you can still complete the project on time. If the latest finish time is the ninth day or earlier, you're behind schedule.

By selecting the action steps that must precede other action steps, and at the same time identifying those which can be carried out simultaneous to other actions, you identify the shortest possible implementation plan for your project. This longest set of consecutive tasks is known as the "critical path" of a project. It should include all of the tasks that must be carried out consecutively, but none of the tasks that can be carried out during the same time as other tasks on the critical path.

In order to accomplish the project on schedule, the critical path must be maintained as scheduled. That's one of the benefits of initiating a process before the latest start date. Should any unanticipated delays occur in your critical path, you can use the buffer time to bring the process back onto the critical path. Once you use this tool a few times, you will find it much less intimidating than it may initially appear. Once you become relaxed with it, you'll wonder how you ever planned a project without it!

DISTINCTIVE TQM CONCEPTS

Total Quality Management, explained in general, is a relatively simple premise. Its institution in an organization, however, is a far more complex endeavor than some people realize. Organizations that have employed TQM for years or even decades have pioneered the development of several groups of actions that can be applied by any organization, regardless of size. Three such action groups are described in this section: Hoshin Planning, Quality Function Deployment, and Daily Management.

To begin with, however, let's review some of the basic foundation actions for every TQM organization. An organization's **MISSION, VISION**, and the **CRITICAL PROCESSES** are important blocks in the foundation of any successful TQM effort.

The mission created by an organization should reflect the organization's purpose for existing. The identification of the organization's customers and the determination of which customer needs will be met and how, should be identified in the mission statement. It is difficult, if not impossible, to implement TQM without a clearly stated mission.

ORGANIZATIONAL MISSION

A clear perception of purpose allows the organization to precisely focus its efforts for effective, constant change. It provides the basis for managed growth by furnishing a more effective means of evaluating competitors, identifying market trends, and creating innovative methods for pleasing your customers. An organization that tries to fulfill every need of every customer will never develop the intense focus necessary to truly innovate for its customers. A mission statement creates a commitment to an area of endeavor specific enough to allow for innovation and quality.

As an example of a mission statement, consider the authors' mission for this text:

"THE MISSION OF TQM, A BASIC TEXT IS TO PROVIDE A SINGLE VOLUME, COMPREHENSIVE, PLAIN LANGUAGE TEXT DESCRIBING THE ELEMENTS AND TOOLS OF TOTAL QUALITY MANAGE- MENT."

Many organizations have created a mission statement which is documented in its files, yet not identifiable in the actual business operation. A sincere organizational mission statement can be immediately reiterated by any member of that organization, and should be the identified origin of every task performed within that organization.

Generally considered one of the first steps in establishing a TQM culture, the creation of a sincere, conscientiously developed mission statement can generate the creative momentum needed to begin your TQM journey.

ORGANIZATIONAL VISION

Too often, we approach life as a plodding series of independent daily endeavors. The organization's future is considered only in terms of variations in market share. When asked what the organization will look like ten years into the future, the CEO might claim that "the market will make that decision for us!"

TQM postulates that our own vision of the future has a tendency to become a self-fulfilling prophecy. We get what we believe we deserve: We become that which we see ourselves becoming. Because this premise has validity, it is absolutely necessary for a TQM organization to formally create a **VISION** of its future self.

A vision should be developed with the mission clearly in mind, and should paint a picture of the organization in the future, once the organizational mission has been realized. It is a description of the organization in the ideal state.

By creating an attainable, challenging vision, an organization creates a destination. TQM, conscientiously instituted, will allow the same organization to devise a road map which will identify a route to that destination.

Consistent with the text mission detailed on the preceding page, the authors' vision is:

> **"TQM , A BASIC TEXT IS USED DAILY BY ORGANIZATIONS THROUGHOUT THE WORLD TO CREATE CUSTOMER-ORIENTED, CONTINUOUS IMPROVEMENT PROCESSES."**

CRITICAL PROCESSES

The illustration used to describe the affinity diagram in the MP Tools section, involved the use of the affinity to identify the critical processes of a small bakery shop owner. **CRITICAL PROCESSES ARE THOSE RELATIVELY FEW, GENERAL ACTIONS THAT MUST BE ACCOMPLISHED TO SATISFY ONE'S CUSTOMERS.**

Each position in an organization will have identifiable critical processes (CP's). While no two positions will have identical CP's, all CP's should display certain basic characteristics or attributes. Those attributes are defined in *Making Daily Management Work*; Collett, Colletti, DeMott, Hoffherr, and Moran; available through GOAL/QPC. Dr. Casey Collett indicates in Chapter 3 of that text that **CRITICAL PROCESSES ARE:**

• **FEW IN NUMBER** (usually 5-10),

• **LINKED**, both horizontally and vertically within the organization,

- **CAPABLE OF BEING MAPPED** or diagrammed (flowcharted),

- **MEASURABLE**,

- **IMPROVABLE**.

The tasks required to fulfill a position's critical processes should account for approximately 75% to 80% of the position-holders time.

The executive level of an organization should be the first to identify his/her CP's. Because the position of owner/CEO has the most general obligation for the success of the organization, that level's CP's will usually be less specific than the CP's for the position of first-level supervisor, for example. Regardless of the level of generality, every level's CP's should display the attributes described above.

Next, in a cascading effect, the organization will begin to identify CP's for those positions that are direct reports to the top executive. Each position in the organization will eventually have formally prepared critical processes. As Dr. Collett points out, the critical processes for all jobs within the organization "are linked together to make up a product or service delivery system that serves the organization's customers."

The CP identification procedure is relatively simple, yet requires careful analysis of the "customer" groups for each position. If the cascade down of CP identification is successful, each level in the organization positively complements all other levels. With CP's identified throughout the organization, each person is able to focus her/his attention to those issues and tasks which most directly support the organization's vision.

Critical processes take the age-old "job description" to a new dimension. Unlike the job-description format of generic obligations, critical processes are clear directions to success for each position.

HOSHIN PLANNING

The term "Hoshin Planning" identifies a management style that employs the concepts and tools of TQM to identify driving or breakthrough issues for the organization, and that creates **ACTION PLANS FOR EVERY MEMBER OF THE ORGANIZATION TO ACCOMPLISH HIS/HER PORTION OF THOSE BREAKTHROUGH ISSUES**. Hoshin Planning is a process in which all members of the organization participate at some level. It is customer driven, data based, and mission and vision focused. In summary, Hoshin Planning is the implementation of true Total Quality Management.

While the Japanese term "Hoshin" is directly translated as "policy" or "target," the word is just as often used synonymously with "breakthrough issue(s)" for an individual or organization. For example, you may hear a particular member of a TQM organization state that her "Hoshin" for the year is the preparation of an effective customer response system. That Hoshin could be traced upward through the organization to the highest level, and specifically detailed as one aspect of the overall organizational breakthrough issue (or Hoshin) for the year.

The general process of Hoshin Planning involves the identification of relatively short-term breakthrough goals by the organizational administration, often with the input of all levels in the organization. The MP Tools are the primary implements in this process. The same tools are used to create sets of more specific goals for each division or member in the organization.

While the Hoshin plan creates relatively short-term goals, the process for achieving those goals is monitored and evolved continually. A constant change TQM format allows for long term planning, while at the same time creates an atmosphere of constant change and improvement. Hoshin reviews are conducted on a regular basis; monthly, weekly, and even daily.

A properly functioning Hoshin Plan creates alignment throughout the organization. Each division or employee knows that the completion of his/her job supports the efforts of all members in the organization, whether horizontally (people or divisions performing similar activities) or vertically (groups or individuals above and below, on the organizational structure).

In businesses of any size, employees benefit psychologically from the knowledge that their input is valued and wanted. Productivity, job satisfaction, and loyalty are common characteristics of TQM organization members/groups. The Hoshin Planning process improves these positive attributes by increasing every member's awareness of the purpose and value of the individual's efforts.

QUALITY FUNCTION DEPLOYMENT (QFD)

Often, organizations interpret the concept of "satisfying the customer" to involve soliciting customers' evaluations, both positive and negative, and using that data to create a better quality product or service. There certainly is nothing wrong with the intent of this process, but it assumes the initial production of a service or product with an uncertain capability of meeting the customers's needs. The product or service may seem like a great idea to Research and Development, or the business owner, but nobody is really certain what the customer response will be until the customer receives the product/service and reacts.

QFD IS A FORMAT OF PRODUCT/SERVICE DEVELOPMENT WHICH IS BASED ON INCORPORATING THE "VOICE OF THE CUSTOMER" INTO EVERY STAGE OF DESIGN, DEVELOPMENT, AND PRODUCTION.

Traditionally, business has developed new products based upon identification of general trends in public interest. A product is developed which the business hopes will meet the needs or capture the interest of the public. A QFD approach to product development includes the same evaluation of current or projected public interest, but continues to base each level of research, design, development, and production on the product characteristics which will meet and exceed the expectations of the customer. Key components of the prospective product are identified and independently evaluated in terms of the customer need or expectation as it applies to the function of that particular component. Quality characteristics are developed for each of those components, and production methods are formulated to deploy the customer-voiced quality characteristic into each key component.

For example, a QFD process for developing a portable microwave oven would include not only the size of the unit, but the reasons the customer wants a portable oven. In addition, an analysis would be made of the desired characteristics of such a unit; including ease of use, reliability, safety, optimum size, minimum weight, etc., all based on meeting the needs of the customer, not the capacity of your current production process.

The components of your portable microwave oven would be evaluated in regard to the role each plays in pleasing the customer, and a determination is made about quality characteristics needed for that component. Raw material selection and production plans for that component are selected in terms of assuring that component's ability to meet or exceed the customer's expectation, not their initial expense.

By the time the QFD planning process is completed, you have already created an assurance of customer satisfaction. All customer-desired characteristics have been evaluated and incorporated into the product plan. All components in the product will perform in a manner that is convenient, efficient, and pleasing to the customer. In essence, you have come as close as humanly possible to guarantying success for your product.

The phrase "Daily Management," in essence, describes the most effective indicator of the health of a Total Quality Management business. A group of lofty general objectives and Hoshin activities do nothing to improve the quality of products and services if they aren't implemented into the most basic fiber of the organization. A daily management application of TQM assures that the relatively tiny daily advances toward the organization's mission and vision take place as necessary.

DAILY MANAGEMENT

A text entitled *Daily Management*, authored by John W. Moran, Ph.D.; Casey Collett, Ph.D.; and Claudette C. Cote, Ph.D., has been published by GOAL/QPC. The text details a process of establishing a formal procedure for monitoring the efficiency of daily actions in an organization.

The most effective daily management systems display an organization-wide awareness of the Quality Control and Management and Planning Tools, and an ongoing application of the appropriate tools throughout the organization. It also requires a firm understanding of every customer's expectations of the organization. When there is a difference between the organization's product/service quality and the level of quality expected by the customer, the tools are applied to identify the causes of inadequate quality and the actions necessary to improve the organization's processes.

Daily Management, the text, illustrates specialized matrices that can be used to compare customer expectations with your organization's quality capacity, given your current processes. By identifying the difference, if any, between customer expectation and process capacity, an organization can begin to make clear, concise plans for process improvements. This constant improvement format is the hallmark of a healthy TQM system.

The process of daily management is simply conducting business with a vigilant eye on Total Quality.

BENCHMARKING

The term "benchmark" originally referred to a fixed surveyor's standard mark from which other points could be measured. In relation to business management, **BENCHMARKING IS THE PROCESS OF SEEKING THE "BEST PRACTICES" OF OTHER ORGANIZATIONS, IMPROVING THEM TO A NEXT-GENERATION QUALITY LEVEL, AND IMPLEMENTING THE NEW "BEST PRACTICES."** A.T.&T., Ford, IBM, Motorola, and Xerox are just a few of the hundreds of organization that maintain formal benchmarking activities. Many organizations have recognized the immense value in learning from others, rather than working independently to recreate existing technologies.

The most obvious form of benchmarking involves emulating the practices of other, similar organizations. It is often most effective to begin benchmarking activities with analyses of only direct competitors. This allows a fledgling benchmarking group to initiate process improvements in relation to known and familiar operations.

Mature benchmarking includes seeking out the world's best practices for the areas needing improvement. The most effective benchmarkers, however, are creative analyzers of processes, and look beyond their immediate professional paradigm. As an example, corporate giant, Xerox, benchmarked the successful mail order firm of L.L. Bean in relation to efficiently and accurately filling customer orders.

Both production and service organizations have created quality momentum by benchmarking production processes, service quality metrics, employee benefit practices, and literally hundreds of other processes.

EPILOGUE

I n many fictional literary works, the epilogue is used to inform the reader of the future of the work's characters. Perhaps that convention is not totally inappropriate in this case.

You are the primary character in this work. You are now aware of the meaning and value of establishing a customer oriented mission and future vision of your organization. You are familiar with the tools which will help you display data, solve problems, and establish meaningful plans. Having a sound concept of TQM in its entirety, you have the capacity to create a future full of profound accomplishment, if you choose.

Your path toward Total Quality will never become a meandering maze, it will never lack challenge, and it will never end. Total Quality, like perfection, is a concept we can never reach, but toward which we should always strive.

Perform a Total Quality act today! Seek out the input of a customer, identify your critical processes, create a mission. A small step today can yield vast future benefits.

Become the character that this book is intended to describe. Make your future as bright as it can possibly be. Exhibit and demand Total Quality in every aspect of your professional life.

APPENDIX A

GROUP AND
TEAM TOOLS

■ ■ ■ ■ ■ ■

There are a variety of methods of developing problem-solution formats in a group setting. The tools described in this appendix are two of the formats that are employed by TQM organizations to generate ideas in group interactions, and to reach group consensus.

BRAINSTORMING

BRAINSTORMING: generally refers to a group of individuals providing creative options to the resolution of a problem. The value of group process in generating new ideas is unquestioned. The procedure by which we can most effectively employ a brainstorming activity, however, is not as well known. Brainstorming is most effective when:

1. Everyone in the group agrees on the problem to be addressed,

2. All members of the group participate,

3. All group members agree that every suggestion, however unique, has potential value and agrees not to ridicule any individual or idea,

4. All suggestions are recorded verbatim, and not interpreted by anyone other than the person making the suggestion,

5.   No one member of the group, regardless of his/her position in the organization, may control the flow of ideas,

6.   Truly unique ideas are especially valued.

       The brainstorming process should be a relatively quick activity, completed within 15 minutes or less for most applications. Don't stop while group members are actively adding new ideas, but don't continue the process until the members feel forced to "make up" ideas rather than produce them spontaneously.

NOMINAL GROUP TECHNIQUE:
(BRAINSTORMING WITH PRIORITIES)

This is a group technique that allows a group to identify a priority ranking for a list of issues. Rather than simply debating until the most tenacious or loudest member decides which item is the most important, the nominal group technique provides a format by which every member of the group has equal input.

The basic principle is quite simple. As a team, make a list of the potentially important options (causes of a particular problem, items to be purchased with limited funds, etc.). Once the list is composed, display the options so each group member can see them. Identify each option with a letter (A, B, C, etc.). Have each group member write the option letters on a piece of paper like this:

A._____
B._____
C._____
etc.

Assuming your group has identified 6 options, and each member has prepared a list of the option letters (A through F), have each group member write a "6" (because you have 6 options) beside the option letter that each feels is the most important option. Next, each member will write a "5" beside the next most important option. Continue until each member has completed her/his own list, which will look something like this:

A. 4
B. 1
C. 6
D. 3
E. 5
F. 2

In this illustration, the team member considered option C to be the most important option, and option B to be the least important.

Once each member has completed his/her list, make a master list comprised of all the members prioritized lists. With a group of four members, the master list might look like this:

A. 4,3,1,2 = 10
B. 1,1,3,3 = 8
C. 6,4,5,4 = 19
D. 3,6,4,1 = 14
E. 5,2,2,6 = 15
F. 2,5,6,5 = 18

The number to the right of the list is the sum of all the priority ratings for each option.

With the master list compiled, the group has completed the nominal group technique. The option with the highest numerical score was option C with 19 points. A close second was option F, which had a score of 18. These two options should be considered the most important issues, with all the other options identified in declining position of importance, based on their numerical score.

APPENDIX B
DEMING'S FOURTEEN POINTS

Dr. W. Edwards Deming institutionalized the concepts of statistical process control (SPC) via the use of the basic statistical tools (Quality Control or QC Tools). It soon became very clear to him that organizational improvement through the use of SPC, alone, was short lived.

The missing cohesive element, he concluded, was a dedicated management philosophy. One that would create an organizational environment for continuous, unending improvement. Over a period of years, Dr. Deming has formulated a total of 14 management mandates which he believes constitutes just such a dedicated management philosophy.

Dr. Deming's 14 points include a recommendation for organizations to redefine their purpose for existing, to move away from short term profit and toward innovation and improvement. (Point 1); a mandate to institute a new quality philosophy, one not tolerant of poor quality (Point 2); a realignment of processes to prevent defects rather than an inspection procedure to delete mistakes after they've been made (Point 3); a recommendation that businesses consider quality, rather that just price, as a primary determiner for purchasing materials and sub-units (Point 4); a reminder to never accept any level of quality as "good enough" (Point 5); the declaration that workers require adequate training in order to perform quality work (Point 6); a mandate for management to "lead" rather than use negative disincentives (Point 7); a reminder that management must create a non-threatening environment that supports inquiry by employees and increases the likelihood that employees won't perform poor quality work because they are afraid to ask for help (Point 8); a suggestion to create an organizational environment that increases cooperation and communication among departments and divisions (Point 9); a reminder that cheer leader-like management doesn't really motivate workers (Point 10); a mandate to eliminate numerical quotas for production, since they tend to create an orientation on quantity rather than quality (Point 11); a reminder that employees **WANT** to perform quality work, and that it's management's job to reduce barriers to quality (Point 12); the fact that managers and workers need training and education in the concepts of quality to perform quality work (Point 13); and a statement that management must create a plan to institute and continue the organization's pursuit of quality.

The following is an abbreviated list of Dr. Deming's 14 points:

1. Create constancy of purpose.

2. Adopt the new philosophy.

3. Cease dependence on mass inspection to achieve quality.

4. End the practice of awarding business on price tag alone. Instead, minimize total cost, often accomplished by working with a single supplier.

5. Improve constantly the system of production and service.

6. Institute training on the job.

7. Institute leadership.

8. Drive out fear.

9. Break down barriers between departments.

10. Eliminate slogans, exhortations, and numerical targets.

11. Eliminate work standards (quotas) and management by objective.

12. Remove barriers that rob workers, engineers, and managers of their right to pride of workmanship.

13. Institute a vigorous program of education and self-improvement.

14. Put everyone in the company to work to accomplish the transformation.

APPENDIX C
PLAN-DO-CHECK-ACT (PDCA) CIRCLE

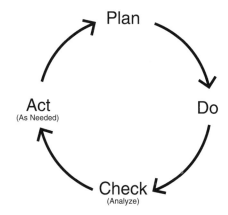

Plan

Do

Check
(Analyze)

Act
(As Needed)

As discussed on page 9 (Element VII of The Ten Element Implementation) the Plan-Do-Check-Act circle represents the process of establishing continuous improvement in an organization.

Employing the PDCA circle in an organization is analogous to breathing for the individual. If the individual ceases to respire, (s)he ceases to exist. If an organization fails to constantly evaluate and modify its processes it, too, will initiate its own obsolescence. A detailed understanding of the PDCA circle is a basic tenet of TQM.

The initiation of the PDCA begins with the "P," PLAN. The planning may involve a large-scale organizational review of operations, or a small-scale, individual unit plan to better carry out a relatively simple task. Regardless of the scale of a process, it should be subjected to constant scrutiny.

While most people consider "planning" to be something that only takes place before a new process is initiated, it should be more generally applied to the idea of constant evaluation as well.

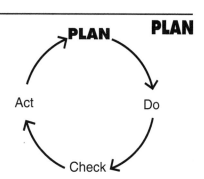

PLAN

PLAN

Act

Do

Check

A plan is any idea that might improve a process, whether it occurs at the point the process is first begun, or at any point later.

Whether the "plan" is a plan to initiate a new process or a plan to improve an existing one, it should be based upon customer needs; and resolve to more effectively fulfill the organization's mission. A plan to alter a hospital's process of scheduling use of the surgery arenas, for example, should be identified in terms of better fulfilling some aspect of the hospital's formal mission statement. Likewise, a small bookstore considering a change in its method of ordering periodicals should base that decision on its mission. If a planned change cannot be tied, in some way, to a more effective fulfillment of the organization's mission, it probably isn't worth consideration.

As an aspect of being mission-consistent, a plan should be based upon clearly identifiable customer needs. The customer needs may have been solicited through questionnaires, they may be the product of customer complaints, or suggestions offered by customers.

The plan should next translate the customer-voiced needs into organizational language. A baseball mitt manufacturer, for example, may clearly hear the customer say, "I need a fielder's mitt that's broken-in when I buy it." The organizational translation of that customer need may be, "Our fielder's mitts need to be constructed of material that is pliable and flexible even before it's subjected to repeated manipulation."

Once translated into organizational language, the customer need becomes a more identifiable target. Raw material choices, manufacturing procedures, service standards, etc. can be effectively established. A specific plan can be prepared relating to a change in the process that will probably result in a product which better meets the needs of the customer.

A final aspect of the plan is the establishment of standards for evaluating the effectiveness of the new process. Only by knowing beforehand what the plan is intended to accomplish, can an organization determine if its planned change has been successful. This includes the identification of an evaluation format, which will allow for the collection of meaningful data about the effectiveness of the plan, once implemented.

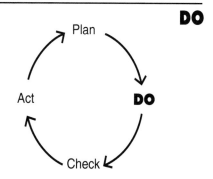

DO

With the mission-consistent, customer-oriented plan prepared, the organization is ready to put the plan into action. It is generally recommended that the new plan be implemented, initially, on a limited scale. This allows for the opportunity to implement the change without committing to a full scale conversion which may not, in spite of the careful planning, be effective. Data, relating to the pre-established standards for determining success, should be conscientiously gathered and evaluated throughout the "DO" stage.

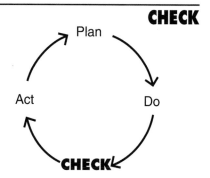

CHECK

The term "CHECK" is sometimes replaced with "Study." The concept is the same; review the gathered data to determine if the planned and implemented change has created the quality improvement intended.

A change may be as successful as hoped. It may also be more or less effective than was anticipated. The evaluation of products and data produced by the changed process may reveal unexpected peripheral benefits, or may identify unanticipated problems in other areas. The "CHECK" should be organization-wide, to reduce the likelihood that a hastily employed change, which initially looked great, will create more problems than it solves.

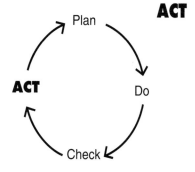

ACT

This step in the never-ending PDCA process involves deciding what to do with the product of the quality experiment. Depending upon the evaluated "success" of the monitored process, you may choose to:

• Run through a second PDCA, changing one or more variables, to see if the process can be made more effective, —or—

• "Standardize" the new, successful process into all production lines, work areas, etc. This constitutes the variation of the PDCA known as the "S" DCA.

Regardless of the choice of actions, the next step is the continued solicitation of the reaction of the customer to the product or service. The process has come "full circle," and is at the "PLAN" point once again.

A never-ending process, the PDCA shouldn't be considered a constant burden, but rather an indication that the organization is still breathing, still transforming to meet the ever-changing needs of the customer.

APPENDIX D
THE TQM WHEEL

G OAL/QPC frequently illustrates the elements of TQM in a circle, known as the TQM Wheel. The TQM Wheel depicts all the basic concepts of TQM, and displays the relationship of each element (Figure 81).

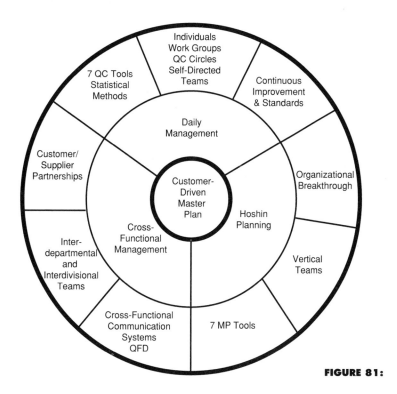

FIGURE 81:

The center of the TQM Wheel is, of course, "the customer." Customer satisfaction drives every aspect of a TQM organizational plan. The three basic segments of the remainder of the circle are Cross Functional Management, Hoshin Planning, and Daily Management. Hoshin Planning tends to be an executive-level obligation. Once a "breakthrough" objective is identified, vertical teams apply the Management and Planning Tools to identify organizational breakthrough actions.

Hoshin Planning focuses the organization on change; productive, constant change. Cross Functional Management involves the use of teams that employ the QC Tools to solve problems. Teams are comprised of representatives of various functions in the organization, and are involved in all phases of Quality Function Deployment, from soliciting the customers' input, to the design and production of new products to meet those customers' needs.

Cross Functional Management implies a "horizontal integration" of various components of the organization, and reinforces the necessity of effective information flow throughout the organization.

Daily Management involves the use of all team and group formats, and employs all the TQM statistical tools. It is the managing of day-to-day actions to create constant movement toward the fulfillment of the organization's mission and vision. All changes that establish higher levels of productivity are standardized, becoming a new basic level of quality.

The GOAL/QPC, TQM Wheel is a condensed and concise illustration of the multiple elements of a comprehensive TQM business management format. As you read through this text, each of the segments of the wheel will be explained in greater detail. Once you have completed the entire text, the TQM Wheel will provide a simple, visual format by which you can summarize Total Quality Management for others.

APPENDIX E
SEEKING CUSTOMER INPUT

Throughout this, and any other text relating to effective managing, you are challenged to create and continuously improve processes to better meet the needs of your customers. Every plan or strategy should be oriented toward a customer-spoken need. Matrices are often used to determine how each part of an organization's activities meets specific customer needs. Clearly, the issue of seeking and effectively utilizing customer needs is basic to total quality.

Customer needs are best spoken by the customer, yet it is amazing how few organizations actually solicit direct customer response. Some business managers feel that asking customers for input is an imposition, or that the organization knows what the customer wants without asking. In fact, the long-term success of any business or organization is determined by its ability to finely tune the organizational processes to **EFFECTIVELY** meet the customers' needs. To assume those needs, or to fail to solicit them because the customer might be "put out," places the organization at an immediate disadvantage to any competitor who **DOES** aggressively seek that input.

Most customers appreciate being asked for their opinion about the services or products for which they spend their hard-earned money. Study after study has shown that most people will not complain about a product or service until they are very dissatisfied; and even then, many will not complain directly to the producer/retailer, but will simply begin doing business with a competitor. Those same studies show that those customers **DO** complain, only the complaint is expressed to their friends and associates. The negative effect of a dissatisfied customer extends far beyond the loss of a single, current customer.

Since the customers' input is basic to TQM, it is the unwavering opinion of the authors that every organization should establish formats for aggressively and continuously seeking that input. There are many different methods of obtaining customer input. This section will briefly discuss some of the most common and effective.

CUSTOMER COMPLAINT FORMS

This most basic customer response tool is inherently the least effective individual method of obtaining meaningful customer input. To begin with, it assumes that unhappy customers will take the time to complete a written complaint. Additionally, it automatically provides only negative feedback. Calling the same "box on the wall" a customer **COMMENT** format rarely increases the quality or quantity of data.

Soliciting the input of distressed customers is an important aspect of a comprehensive customer data collection process, however. And, sometimes the "box on the wall" will gather data which would otherwise be lost.

While it may not be necessary to get rid of the complaint box, it is far more effective to seek out all kinds of customer input using one or both of the following customer information processes.

CUSTOMER SURVEYS

Every contact a member of your organization has with a customer is an opportunity to collect customer data. Surveys may be formal, involving printed forms requesting customer profile information such as age, gender, income, marital status, vehicles owned, or any other data that would be relevant to the organization in terms of identifying its customer type. Such a detailed survey might also include objective response questions relating to the customer's perception of the quality of service or product. It could also solicit data relating to the service/product improvements the customer would like to see incorporated in the future.

Survey information is sometimes collected informally, as well. When a customer makes a statement relating to a product or service, for example, the employee to whom it was made may simply make a note of the comment, but not make further inquiry into the matter. While **ALL** customer-generated information is valuable, the informal procedure is far less useful and reliable, due to the fact that the comment must be interpreted without further input from the customer.

Some organizations employ printed surveys which are mailed to customers. It is appropriate to include a stamped return envelope, and some businesses even include a discount coupon or other benefit as a reward for the customers' time. The weakness of mailed surveys involves the notoriously low return rate. Armida Dorso, the Guest Services Manager for a large hotel in Albuquerque, New Mexico developed a format that increased the guest survey form response by approximately 800%! She simply included, with each guests survey form, a poem indicating that each returned survey would be placed in a monthly drawing which would net one lucky respondent a check for $50.00.

Telephone surveys vastly increase the response ratio and allow the surveyor to ask clarifying questions.

CUSTOMER FOCUS GROUPS

In order to obtain more detailed customer input, a few progressive organizations utilize the focus group format. With some variation, the format involves inviting specific customers to a meeting to discuss the quality of a product and/or service provided by an organization. The meeting may be held at the place of business, or at a neutral location (a local conference location or restaurant for example). Some organizations prefer to have their own representatives facilitate the meeting, others choose to have an independent facilitator or consultant conduct the meeting. The benefit of having an "outsider" facilitate the meeting is the objectivity implied. Some customers will be more open and honest about their feelings if they know the facilitator is not directly associated with the organization being discussed.

As with the written survey, it is usually appropriate to have some benefit afforded those who agree to attend a focus group meeting. That may mean buying them dinner, or providing some other benefit directly associated with the business. The potential value of the information makes the cost of a few dinners a sound investment.

While the type of information solicited depends largely upon the kind of organization that sponsors the focus group, the basic idea is to solicit input regarding the quality of the organization's service/product **FROM THE CUSTOMERS' PERSPECTIVE**. The focus group format allows the facilitator to ask follow-up questions and to request greater detail or examples, none of which is easily accomplished with mailed surveys.

Though usually the most expensive, in terms of dollars per customer involved, the focus group produces the most detailed customer data. By conducting a series of customer focus groups, an organization can identify its success in relation to various groups of customers.

Once raw customer data is collected, the QC Tools can be utilized to display and analyze the customers' evaluation of the organization's products/services. The MP Tools may also be used to combine the statistical data with the specialized knowledge of members of the organization. The combination of clearly-spoken customers' needs and a competent, vision-oriented organization assure processes which will most effectively meet those customer needs.

The most effective customer input process involves soliciting data from **EVERY** customer. Obviously, that will be easier if you sell luxury cars than if you deliver residential mail nationwide. The option to surveying all customers is to survey a representative cross-section. Consult other texts, other organizations, or consultants for more detailed information about soliciting the voice of the customer.

GLOSSARY

ACTIVITY NETWORK
An MP Tool which can be used to identify the actions involved in a process, and the earliest and latest start and finish time for each action in relation to a desired process completion time.

AFFINITY DIAGRAM
An MP Tool which allows the user to create natural groupings from a large number of apparently unrelated pieces of data.

BARBELL CHART
A QC Tool which displays the distribution of variation in a process; also known as a histogram.

BENCHMARKING
The practice of improving your organization's processes to reflect the most significant advancements made by other organizations.

CAUSE AND EFFECT DIAGRAM
Also known as the fishbone diagram, this QC Tool provides a format for investigating all of the potential effectors which might be causing a problem in a process.

CHECK SHEET
A simple QC Tool used to coordinate samples of data, a tally sheet.

CONTROL CHART
A special use run chart with statistically calculated upper and lower control limits, one of the traditional QC Tools.

CRITICAL PROCESSES
A relatively small number (about 5-10) of the general actions which should account for a majority of an individual's time.

CROSS-FUNCTIONAL TEAM
A team comprised of individuals representing different functions within an organization (e.g., R&D, production, sales, etc.).

DAILY MANAGEMENT
The process of identifying and carrying out those specific, daily actions that constitute incremental advancement toward the organization's mission and vision.

DESCENDING BAR CHART
A QC Tool which employs bars, in decreasing heights, to display the frequency of different factors under investigation; also known as a Pareto chart.

EXECUTIVE STEERING COMMITTEE
A group of organizational members identified to oversee the implementation and maintenance of TQM within an organization.

FISHBONE DIAGRAM
A cause and effect diagram.

FIVE-YEAR PLAN
A long range organizational plan.

FLOW CHART
A QC Tool used to illustrate the steps in a progressive process.

FUNCTIONAL TEAM
A team made up of individuals who perform similar functions in an organization.

HISTOGRAM
Also known as a barbell Chart, a QC Tool which displays the distribution of variation in a process.

HOSHIN
A term generally associated with an organization's relatively short-term, high impact goals; also known as organizational breakthrough.

INTERNAL CUSTOMER

Anyone in your organization who is affected by your efforts; whether they supply you with information/products, or receive them from you.

INTERRELATIONSHIP DIGRAPH

An MP Tool which displays a number of issues, and identifies the cause/effect relationships among them.

MANAGEMENT AND PLANNING TOOLS

Also known as the MP Tools; a group of tools which allows the user to utilize concepts, ideas, and other nonspecific data to create useful and statistically valid plans and strategies.

MATRIX

Any chart format which displays two or more variables, as well as the presence and/or level of interrelationship of those variables (e.g., L-shaped matrix, T-shaped matrix, etc.).

MISSION

A statement identifying an organization's purpose for existing.

PARETO CHART

Also known as a descending bar chart; a QC Tool which employs bars, in decreasing heights, to display the frequency of different factors.

PRIORITIZATION MATRIX

An L-shaped matrix which displays a number of criteria on one axis, and a number of options on the other axis. The final prioritization matrix identifies the best option(s) based on the listed criteria.

PROCESS DECISION PROGRAM CHART (PDPC)

An MP Tool which employs a tree diagram to identify specific actions which should constitute the accomplishment of a goal, identifies the probable problems which may arise at given points, and creates contingency plans, should those problems occur.

QUALITY CONTROL TOOLS

Also known as QC Tools; a set of tools designed to allow the user to visually display data, or analyze processes.

QUALITY FUNCTION DEPLOYMENT

A method used to create customer satisfaction by modifying every production process to most effectively create customer-desired characteristics in the final product.

RUN CHART
A QC Tool which displays variations in a process over time.

SCATTER DIAGRAM
A QC Tool which provides a display of the relationship of two factors, and creates a visual display of the cause and effect relationship between those factors.

TEN ELEMENT IMPLEMENTATION MODEL™
A TQM overview format developed by GOAL/QPC. The ten elements begin with the decision to implement TQM, and proceed through a series of logical steps to create a well established TQM management format.

TQM WHEEL
The TQM wheel is a visual representation of all the major elements of TQM.

TREE DIAGRAM
An MP Tool used to create a group of specific actions which constitute the accomplishment of a more general goal.

VISION
An organizational statement which depicts the organization in the perfect state of function.

INDEX